WITCHES, ORANGES AND SLINGERS

HALF A CENTURY ON MALLORCA

ELENA DAVIS

TRAFFORD

Note for Librarians: a cataloguing record for this book that includes Dewey Decimal Classification and US Library of Congress numbers is available from the Library and Archives of Canada. The complete cataloguing record can be obtained from their online database at:
www.collectionscanada.ca/amicus/index-e.html
ISBN 1-4251-0725-7

Cover illustration by Judith Bledsoe
Cover design by Ivan Feder

With a few exceptions, the names of all persons mentioned in this book have been changed as I should not like to offend most of them.

TRAFFORD

Offices in Canada, USA, Ireland and UK

Book sales for North America and international:
Trafford Publishing, 6E–2333 Government St.,
Victoria, BC v8t 4p4 CANADA
phone 250 383 6864 (toll-free 1 888 232 4444)
fax 250 383 6804; email to orders@trafford.com
Book sales in Europe:
Trafford Publishing (uk) Ltd., Enterprise House, Wistaston Road Business Centre,
Wistaston Road, Crewe, Cheshire cw2 7rp UNITED KINGDOM
phone 01270 251 396 (local rate 0845 230 9601)
facsimile 01270 254 983; orders.uk@trafford.com
Order online at:
trafford.com/06-2483

10 9 8 7 6 5 4 3

TO MICKY

and

MY PARIS FAMILY

EARLY DAYS

It was the best decision of my life: To leave New York and spend four months in Spain on the Mediterranean island of Mallorca, the largest of the Balearics. That was in 1959. It is now 2006, forty-seven years later, and I am still here.

And if a fortune teller had predicted that one day I should hold twenty powers of attorney from property owners here and that I also should own some 10,000 books, I'd have answered, "Get yourself another crystal ball." But that prediction would have been correct.

On the third of April of that year my writer-violinist friend Escha Bledsoe, Mrs. Higgins, her black cocker spaniel named for the ink, and I sailed from New York for France on the S.S. Flandre. We were to stop in Paris, where Escha's daughter lived, before going south to Spain. Escha was returning to her home, which she had so imaginatively decorated, in the valley of Sóller on the northwest coast of Mallorca – a house she called her paradise. It was a heavenly spot in the center of the valley famous for its oranges with the surrounding mountains, the Serra Tramuntana, terraced in silver-green olive trees, and is one of the most beautiful places I have ever known. It was so tranquil, the air so clear and not a sound except bird song and early in the morning the cocks crowing. I have been privileged to enjoy such a fabulous setting for more than half my life.

When they heard of my decision, some of my friends thought that I had lost my mind. And my English father, who had never travelled in his life, asked, "Why don't you take a cruise?"

It wasn't as harebrained an idea as it might have at first seemed, though, as I had some familiarity with the island. Unlike many Americans at that time, I grew up knowing about the existence of Mallorca (or Majorca, as it was then called in English) because my mother had friends who had come here in the 20's. In addition, I had visited Escha in Sóller in 1955 and 1957. Both times I took lessons in Spanish [español], also called Castilian [castellano], which was then the only legal language during General Franco's long regime although the natives spoke Mallorquín among themselves, even if they could not write it.

Escha's experiences on the island went back to 1952 when she had arrived with two colleagues (they were working on radio scripts). They all stayed in a hotel in the port of Sóller, some three kilometers from the center of the town, where Escha paid sixty-nine pesetas (considerably less than half a euro in today's currency) a day for room, complete board and service. After a short while her two companions decided to return to the United States but she stayed on in Villa Rua, a charming two-bedroom house and garden in the La Huerta area between the town and the port. The rent was very modest. The neighbor who came in to do housework asked for four pesetas an hour. This seemed very reasonable, too, but later on Escha learned that the going rate was only two and a half pesetas. It also developed that her rent was four times as much as the previous tenants had paid. Well, it is understandable that it seemed to many of the local people that all foreigners who came from thousands of kilometers away must be rich although in reality she had a very limited income.

Later I also ran into a situation where, as a foreigner, I was overcharged. A hairdresser had been recommended to me. For a shampoo, set and haircut she charged forty-five pesetas, very little by American standards. I was pleased with her work; but when I learned that the Mallorquíns were paying only twenty-five pesetas, the shop lost my custom. I learned something interesting at that hairdresser's: The black hair of many Mallorquín women came out of a bottle.

During Escha's early years on the island, I frequently had to arrange for transfer of dollars from the United States to her account here. The money always took a long time to arrive, and no method of transfer was satisfactory. I tried American Express, personal checks, bank transfers and finally, in desperation, bills which I wrinkled and then wrapped in carbon paper – I had been told that this would protect against theft. One day some weeks after I had sent Escha a personal check which actually reached her and she had cashed, an officer of my bank in New York asked me to see him. He showed me my check. When I looked at him questioningly, he asked, "Will you please sign it." Incredible as it may seem, it had gone through at least two international agencies and, I believe, the Federal Reserve Bank before being returned to my bank – without a signature (fortunately my name was printed on the check).

The postal service here was somewhat erratic. When Escha came here in 1952, I wrote to her regularly, but soon I received letters from her begging me to write, saying she had had no word from me since she had left New York. Again and again I wrote, but for perhaps two months none of my letters reached her. Eventually she accosted the local postman who proudly assured her that he was taking care of all mail addressed to Villa Rua by forwarding it to some address in France where the previous tenants had gone!! Not one of the letters came back. Incidentally, the local post office collected a small "voluntary" donation for each registered letter or C.O.D package for a fund for retired and disabled employees; but as the purpose was good, we did not object.

Much later friends of ours who lived in the port moved from one house to another across the bay, but their postman made it his business to continue to deliver mail to the original house. It took several weeks to correct this situation.

When I was planning my first visit to this country in 1955, I looked forward to the overnight flight to Madrid with some apprehension. I had been to Europe before but by ship and had never taken a seven- or eight-hour flight. It turned out to be a much longer trip than anticipated as we ran into strong winds and had to change direction and make an unscheduled stop at the Portuguese island of Madeira to refuel. We passengers were given a snack, and then we waited for a couple of hours, wondering at the delay. Eventually a van rushed up to the plane to deliver another meal for us. We finally arrived in Madrid in late afternoon instead of in the morning, so I missed having a day to become acquainted with the city. The pilot of the New York-Madrid flight was a passenger on the plane I took to Palma de Mallorca; and as we chatted, he told me that he had been given faulty weather information in the United States. I was American enough then to feel embarrassed.

My bag which held a big fat copy of the preceding Sunday's "New York Times," as well as personal items, never arrived in Palma. After a long correspondence, Iberia Airlines recompensed me for the loss; but I was disappointed not to be able to give Escha a copy of the paper she had not seen for three years. When I came to live here four years later, it took me some months to get over the feeling of missing something very important every Sunday: the wonderful coverage of news, arts, books, theater and all the other informative articles.

Escha met me at the airport in Palma, the capital city, and we taxied across the plain and then over the mountain, the *Coll*, with its sixty-plus hairpin curves (which had isolated Sóller from the rest of Mallorca until the railroad connecting Palma and Sóller was constructed), through the town's main square and on to Villa Rua. Many years ago, before the railroad existed, there was a diligence, or stagecoach, service which used mules; four of them got the vehicle up to the top of the *Coll* where the exhausted animals were exchanged for fresh ones to finish the journey.

Tired though I was after my long trip from New York, I was in a high state of excitement and impatiently waited for my first sight of Escha's little home which, to my amazement, was not on the water's edge. I am sure now that she had never told me it was, but that was how I had visualized it. And the next morning when she took me up to the center of town and I saw its principal square, the Plaza de Calvo Sotelo (but now known as Plaça de Sa Constitució, the name having been changed after Franco's death and from Spanish to Mallorquín), with its many streets radiating out from it, nothing looked as it had in my imagination prior to my visit.

The Church of San Bartolomé, dominating the square, was built in the early thirteenth century but had been modified many times since then. Now the main structure is baroque, but the façade was designed in 1904 by an architect trained by Gaudi, Joan Rubió. Next to it was the impressive Banco Hispano Americano (now, having been taken over by other banks, known as Banco Santander Central Hispano, which had been established in 1889 as the Banco de Sóller by returned wealthy emigrants, many Sollerenses having made fortunes in Puerto Rico and South America.) This building also was designed by Rubió and is known for its arched entrance and forged iron windows.

But the daily open market in the square which existed when Escha arrived had been moved to a new building a few months later.

Almost the first purchase I made that first day on Calle de la Luna (now Carrer de sa Lluna), the most important shopping street constructed above what had been a Moorish water channel), was a pair of *alpargatos*, rope-soled canvas shoes, which I later took back to New York and, inappropriate as they were, happily wore to my office. I later discovered some splendid buildings on that street and on the Gran Via as well as houses dating back to the fourteenth century on some of the narrow lanes and alleys of the town.

A number of things surprised me: For example, our butcher was a woman – in fact, she was just one of many in that line of work. She was skilled but some of the cuts of meat were different from ours. The word *bifstek* was used not only for beef but for a slice of pork or lamb or whatever. And there were big hunks of meat hanging all around the shop and not in the refrigerator. But how good the chicken and pork and eggs were, all from local farms. I realized how modestly some local people had to live only when I saw the women buying just one hundred or two hundred grams of meat chopped up to flavor a *paella* for an entire family. On one occasion I innocently asked what some oval items on a plate were. When the other customers tittered, I suddenly understood that they were bulls' testicles which I had never seen in an American butcher's.

I noticed that the *guardias civiles* [civil guards] all smoked American cigarettes which were much more expensive than the Spanish and I wondered how they could afford them. It was some time before I learned that those were contraband cigarettes and, I was informed on more than one occasion by Mallorquíns, that contraband pharmaceutical drugs also were moved through our mountains. About once every six months or so there was a raid on the *contrabandistas,* but then apparently business went on as usual.

My GP in New York had insisted on my having a number of injections and vaccinations against various diseases she thought might be prevalent here. I am sure none of these precautions was necessary. Outside of bronchitis and rheumatism due to the damp of the Sóller valley, most people here were very healthy and lived, and still live, to a good age. They had to work hard and lacked many comforts, but the atmosphere was clean, and the basic diet of fresh vegetables and fruit, bread, chicken, rice, fresh fish, small quantities of meat and wine, known as the Mediterranean Diet, encouraged good health.

Almost as soon as I arrived at Villa Rua that first visit, I experienced the lack of amenities in Spain compared with the United States. Escha told me that Francisca, the young woman who worked for her then, would launder anything soiled, so I gave her the cotton and synthetic blouse I had traveled in on my flights from New York. In ten or fifteen minutes she proudly handed me a hanger with the blouse beautifully ironed, but obviously not washed. As my Spanish was not up to it, Escha questioned Francisca who replied that of course she had not washed the blouse as she had not wanted the colors to run - in 1955 fast-color fabrics were almost unknown here.

Instead of going to the bank to exchange money at the legal rate of some thirty-eight pesetas to the dollar, you could do better by using one of the money changers in Palma. All the foreigners did this. Although I was a bit nervous about getting involved in such an illegal transaction, the higher return tempted me. I went to Palma to Smiths, a long-established agency which made travel arrangements, helped with official papers, sold house insurance, had an English rental library and, of course, changed foreign currency for pesetas. When I entered the office from the street, Mr Smith greeted me and asked what he could do for me. I looked round, then replied in a low voice that I wanted to change some dollars. He said in a loud voice, "Oh, yes, of course, you want to change dollars. Please come this way."

I expected any minute to feel the heavy hand of the law on my shoulder, but fortunately the transaction was completed without problems, and I walked out a free woman with my pesetas. The first of many devaluations of the peseta that I experienced took place in 1959 when the rate increased to fifty-nine to the dollar; the rate for a pound was about one hundred and eighteen pesetas. The financial black market then more or less disappeared.

Incidentally, though many of us depended on Smiths to arrange tickets and other papers for us, they did let Escha down one day. An emergency arose and she had to leave suddenly for the mainland so phoned them to reserve a place for her on the Palma night ferry that evening. Just before their closing time Escha got to Smiths to pick up her tickets only to face an embarrassed man who admitted he'd forgotten to make the arrangements. He rushed out to the ferry office and fortunately the boat was not full, so Escha was able to make her connections.

One day Escha took me to dinner at the Hotel Guia which had a well deserved reputation for its food. In the 50's and 60's there were few restaurants in the valley, and the Guia was surely the best. It was where Escha used to go almost daily for lunch when she was working on a book and had no time to shop and cook. Her one-dish meal with a glass of wine cost her eighteen pesetas. If she wanted to eat more economically she went to an ordinary restaurant which charged only twelve pesetas. The day I was Escha's guest, we had a full meal with wine and coffee, followed by a *coñac* offered by the host. Her bill was eighty-four pesetas which was fair. Before I left Sóller I returned the invitation. We had a good meal though no final drink was offered. My unitemized bill, a scrap of paper, showed only the outrageous figure of one hundred and twenty-five. The owner had a reputation for being very erratic in his behaviour, so after I took one look at his face which seemed to indicate that he would accept no argument, I paid without a murmur.

This man could be very kind on occasion, however. One

Christmas years later when a group of us were lunching at his restaurant, a couple somewhat the worse for wear came in. They had obviously begun their celebrations early in the day and they continued to drink their lunch. Suddenly the man got up and lurched out leaving his wife. Soon she looked to be in trouble and the host went over to her, helped her with her coat and escorted her to the door where he waited with her until a taxi came. She did not pay for the meal and I am sure he never presented her with a bill.

Following those first few weeks in Mallorca in 1955, I went to Paris for a five-day visit, then a couple of days in London and back home. Our departure from the island did not go as smoothly as hoped. On the way to the airport via neighboring Deià, we stopped for a brief visit with Escha's friends, Beryl and Robert Graves. After checking in at the airport, Escha went to have her passport stamped. A few minutes later she ran over to me and said that she could not leave the country without a *salida*, an exit permit. She had explained to the officers that she had gone to the HQ of the Guardia Civil in Sóller some days before, and they had assured her that she did not need such a document. The officials were not moved. There was nothing for it but for her to rush in to Palma and get a permit there; meanwhile I explained the situation to Air France who removed our bags from the truck on the way to the plane. I then did something foolish but it made me feel better: In my inadequate Spanish I berated the passport officers who sat looking bemused; in those days they were certainly not accustomed to receiving abuse from a member of the public. An hour later Escha returned without the document: the office was closed in the afternoon. (Had we not stopped for that visit in Deià, Escha might just have found the office still open.) Air France changed our tickets for the following day, and we went off to find a reasonable hotel to spend the night.

In 1955 there were not that many hotels in Palma, and in July most of them were fully occupied. We went to three of them with no luck. Finally the taxi driver told us he knew of one on the outskirts of the city which might have a room, and it did. It looked respectable enough and, in addition, I saw sitting at one of the tables outside a man and his young daughter who had given me a ride from the port only two days before when I had missed the Sóller streetcar. But when we checked in, the receptionist did not ask for our passports, which was most unusual. As we were tired we passed up dinner and soon went to bed. First Escha, then I began to scratch. Yes, bedbugs. The window shades in the room facing us in the other wing of the hotel went down, then half an hour or so later they were raised; someone came in to remake the bed and prepare the room, the shades soon went down again, and so on. The room was certainly not being used for overnight sleepers. In addition, the water tank in the lavatory down the hall never stopped running, so Escha turned the water off. That night was certainly not one of the best of my life. And the next day the hotel had our uneaten dinner on our bill – needless to say we refused to pay for it.

On the plane to Paris Air France served us a wonderful lunch, ending with a basket of fruit and cheese which we could not cope with, so we scooped them up and put them into one of our bags to have for a light supper that evening. An American woman whom we had met at the airport and who had been impressed by Escha because she was carrying a book manuscript to be turned over to her agent saw us do this and immediately lost interest in us. This woman and her husband, by the way, had been staying at the Hotel Formentor (chosen, no doubt, because it was the most expensive on the island – their room cost the enormous sum of $15 a day). A few years later when I was living here I went on a day's excursion round the island. We stopped at the Formentor and I was horrified to be charged fifteen pesetas for *Coñac* 103 for which I paid only three pesetas at my bar in Sóller. (Today the price at the bar is sixty-one times as much.) The Formentor, opened in 1929, hosted during the years many famous people, such as, Grace Kelly and Rainier, Gorbachev, Peter Ustinov and dozens of other royals, politicians, movie stars and the like.   It was put on the market in 2000 for the equivalent of approximately $186,279,670, or £81,784,387.

On that first vacation in Mallorca I fell in love with the island and vowed that I would find a way to come back to live here permanently, and my second holiday here confirmed this decision.   But as I had no private income, I knew that I would have to find a way to earn a living if I wanted to make this island my home. Yes, life was cheap by our standards, but eventually my money would run out and I should need an income after that. I could not then imagine what turn my life would take and the numerous activities I should be involved in to ensure that I could make it financially here. And in addition, that I should one day be able to fulfill my dream of being able to buy and read all (well, almost all) the books I wanted to.

During my second holiday visit in 1957 we decided to go to Ibiza for a few days. At that time there were no inter-island flights, so we took the six-hour ferry from Palma on the seventh of June. Our tickets covered chairs on the deck, and in the pleasant weather the voyage was most agreeable. We had reserved a room in a small hotel in San Antonio Abad, as it was then known. The beach was beautiful and unspoiled by hotels or other buildings. On the Sunday we saw many women in traditional dress, and one nursed her baby on the bus to the city of Ibiza. When we checked in at the dock for our return voyage, the official tried to charge us an additional amount, saying the tickets were not correct. I raised my voice and carried on and somehow or other my rudimentary Spanish won the argument. When we were at sea it began to rain, so we went into the first class salon where we had no right to be. But Escha politely greeted the attendant and chatted with her for a few minutes, and there was no problem about our being there. When two German women came in, however, and ignored the attendant, she asked to see their tickets which were not first class and then made them leave. This was only one of a number of incidents which showed local feeling against that nationality at that time.

The entire trip for both of us, including the ferry tickets, hotel for four nights, meals and a few minor purchases, cost 1,630 pesetas, the equivalent then of about forty-three dollars. But, of course, that was forty-nine years ago.

(Incidentally, some thirty-five years later I made another visit to Ibiza in connection with a charitable group with which I was associated, and I not only could not find the *hostal* where we had stayed but the beach and surroundings in San Antonio were unrecognizable. Hotels and apartment houses had sprung up everywhere.)

It seemed very odd that in the Madrid airport after my flight from Palma on my way back to the United States in 1957 we had to go through Customs. . The *guardia civil* pawing through my things – and he did not wear gloves -- apparently was not prepared for women's garters (I wore different clothes in those days); and when mine fell out on the floor, he hastily finished his search. But the American government could also make things difficult for incoming passengers. On one of my visits back to the States to see my mother in Florida in the late 70's our plane stopped at Puerto Rico, and Americans had to make a declaration of their purchases abroad. But I wasn't a returning resident of the United States. I had lived abroad for almost twenty years during which I had bought various items of clothing which I intended to bring back with me to Spain after my visit. I had more than the permitted free allowance for returning Americans but there seemed to be no exception for travellers like me, so I simply "forgot" to list everything.

Now in April, 1959, I was on my way to my big adventure, and Escha was returning after a year away, so we had between us thirty-two suitcases, duffle bags and boxes holding not only clothes and personal effects but also linens, blankets and tools for the house, two typewriters, her violin, a package of records for the record player, a case with supplies for our four-footed friend Mrs. Higgins and other items not available in Spain. (Mrs. Higgins unfortunately disgraced herself on the deck of the ship, but the personnel very kindly made no fuss about it.) The reason I had so many possessions with me is that, though I had been given only a three-month leave of absence and my annual vacation of one month from my job in public relations with the National Foundation for Infantile Paralysis, I had saved enough money to keep me for a year at the then very low cost of living and took with me clothes and necessities for the entire period as I hoped to be able to stay that long.

In order for the dog to enter Spain, we had been told by the Spanish Consulate in New York that we needed some special documents. First, a veterinarian, a friend of mine, filled in a health certificate which we took to the corner cigar store to be notarized. (This may seem odd to non-New Yorkers or non-Americans, but at that time, at any rate, the owner of a tobacco shop-newstand usually was a notary public, and for a very small fee he witnessed signatures and notarized documents. The work of such a person had nothing to do with that of a Spanish notary.) The next day I took the certificate downtown to the Municipal Building for a legalization of some sort. The clerk looked at my document and told me the notary had omitted some words, such as, "before me this day appeared," then asked where the notary was. When I replied that he was uptown, she said with a perfectly straight face, "Why don't you go outside to the phones and call him?" It took me a few seconds to catch on, and I then asked her to repeat the missing phrase, left her office and outside wrote in the necessary words. When I returned and handed the fee and the paper to the clerk, she took them without a word, stamped the document and handed it back to me. This is the kind of thing that has happened to me here, particularly many years ago when matters were handled in a less formal way than now, but I had never before had such an experience in the United States.

The next step was to take the certificate to the Spanish Consulate – but I found it was closed that day so I had to return the next – to have an enormous number of stamps affixed to it. The postscript to this story is that we did not have to show it when we entered Spain. In addition, we had been advised that such a certificate was required for the obligatory registration of the dog in Sóller, so shortly after our arrival I took it to the old town hall, opened in 1733, where a clerk looked at it but appeared puzzled. Finally he found a scrap of paper on which he wrote Mrs. Higgins' name and age, Escha's name, and so on. And that was the end of the health certificate. But if you had a dog as a pet and not as a working animal on a farm, say, you had to pay an annual fee. (In those days you also paid a tax every year on a radio.) Mrs. Higgins lived a good long life but eventually the time came for us to ask the vet to come to put her to sleep. The very pleasant neighboring farmer offered to save us the vet's fee, saying that he would be glad to give the dog a hard blow on the head with his shovel. We delined his offer.

On the day we sailed from America I was in such a state of euphoria that when I tried to introduce one of my closest friends to someone else seeing us off, I literally could not remember her name. We then spent two weeks in Paris with Judith, Escha's daughter, and her family. Fortunately dogs were, and still are, acceptable in hotels, and Mrs. Higgins slept in one of our empty suitcases. When we took the train from Paris, our great number of pieces of baggage caused some commotion in the station. We insisted on having the dog with us in the compartment, but most of the big cases went into the baggage car. Unfortunately, through a misunderstanding when the station official wrote up the complicated papers for them, he included the violin. Escha said she would not let it out of her sight, so that required a second set of documents. By this time the whistle was blowing for the train's departure – French trains always left on time – so we had to run like stuck steers to board, and it moved even before we got to our compartment.

At Port Bou at the border it was necessary to change trains due to the difference then in French and Spanish tracks, and that meant going through Customs. Escha knew a man from the travel agency Marsans who was there and who got us through formalities ahead of everyone else without our having to open anything or show the dog's health certificate which had caused me such trouble. That resulted in some dirty looks directed our way from the other passengers. It also recalled to Escha her first arrival in 1952 when everything she had was opened and examined by the Guardia Civil. Because she knew they were not available in Spain she had packed a good quantity of tampons, which were completely unknown to the *guardias*. She spoke English and French; they spoke only Spanish. It took her a few minutes of very embarrassing gestures to prevent them from ripping open more tampons as they questioned, *"Qué es esto?"* ["What is this?"] before they finally caught on, reddened from their soles to the top of their patent leather hats, slammed shut her trunk and told her to go.

When we arrived in Barcelona and were going through the station, two men approached us and tried to get our attention. Escha told me to ignore them as they were probably trying to sell us something. Fortunately she was wrong. Shortly before I had left New York, I had become friendly with a Spaniard who said he would write to his friends in Barcelona to help us on our arrival. Even though I had given him information on our travel plans, I did not believe that anything would come of his offer. We finally realized who they were and were delighted to accept their assistance. First, they took me around the city – Escha, having visited Barcelona many times, went to one of the public baths where she could rest for some hours. When we were about to enter the cathedral, I hesitated as I had no hat and did not want to offend anyone in a strictly Catholic country; but my new acquaintances shrugged that off and said it didn't matter. I was shocked to see a prominent sign inside the cathedral warning people about thieves.

No taxi driver would take us to the ferry dock with all our luggage and the dog, so the two men went off and found a large kind of wheelbarrow which they loaded, then pushed as we walked down to the ferry. The overnight ferry voyage was uneventful. In Palma de Mallorca two taxis took us to the train station, and on arrival in Sóller Escha was greeted by a number of drivers whom she knew so we had no difficulty in reaching her villa with all our belongings.

SETTLING IN

Then came the reality of settling in and learning how to live under conditions that were primitive compared with those I was familiar with in New York. I was soon to learn that day-to-day living was different from a holiday stay. And while the lack of hot running water was not so important in spring and summer, when I had visited, it certainly would be in the colder months as well as not having adequate heating in a stone house with tiled floors because it is NOT spring all year round on this island. Contrary to what some people believe who have never been here, we do have winters. (I still live without central heating though I have various heaters throughout my house as well as a fine fireplace upstairs in my livingroom – and the building of that fireplace is another story.)

From the above comments, it is probably obvious that I decided long before my four months had passed to stay on longer, so I wrote to my office asking to extend my leave of absence. Not surprisingly, they replied in the negative, and I then had to make a major decision. I sat down with a piece of paper in front of me, headed on the left, "Reasons for returning," and on the right, "Reasons for staying here." There were three or four lines in the lefthand column, but on the right side only the four words, "Because I want to." And so I stayed.

We were not connected to the town's running water. Villa Rua had a huge cistern under the back patio; and after heavy rains had cleaned the roof, we removed a big cork stopper to let the water go down into the *deposito*. A motor sent it up to a tank in the attic and water flowed from that when we opened a faucet.

Other items that were taken for granted in the United States were such things as coffee without caffeine which Escha needed (a concoction of powdered chicory and malt was just about a drinkable substitute) or paper handkerchiefs and towels; and I remember my shock on my first return visit to America at how wasteful people seemed with so many things, ordinary obviously to them but not to me in Spain. Fortunately for me by the time I arrived Escha had found substitutes for certain essentials or, simply, had learned how to live without them. There was a limited supply of canned goods, but we did have wonderful fresh local fruits and vegetables. Only yesterday I saw a carton of limes for sale at my local grocer's and recalled the day forty-some-odd years ago when I asked about this fruit by description ("smaller than a lemon but green") as I did not know the name in Spanish – it is *lima* which I might have guessed, but I am sure many local people then were just as ignorant of the name as I was. The young woman I was speaking to asked if I were thinking of a *pomelo* [grapefruit]. Incidentally, this fruit was not very popular which was not surprising as any available at that time were thick-skinned and full of seeds.

It was many years later before we enjoyed imported products. As a result, when we had friends in for drinks we had to use our imagination in the preparation of bits and pieces to go with them or, rather, Escha had already done so long before

I came. Whiskey was out of the question and tonic water was unknown, but many other drinks were available, including a local one called *palo* which is made from carob beans (also known as St John's bread). Most people either like or hate it. I am among the former.

Another local drink (often homemade) is *hierbas.* The principal ingredient is aniseed, but there are many other herbs used and they are left in the bottle. Everyone seems to have a different recipe, and it can be very strong. My preference is for a mixture of the dry and the sweet. Mallorquíns also like a drink called *horchata*, particularly in summer, made from *chufas* [tigernuts], which is sweet and nutritious, but to the best of my knowledge it has never been taken up by many foreigners.

It wasn't difficult to be seduced by the beautiful valley of Sóller and its tree-covered mountains, with its scenic port not very far away.. Sunsets were magnificent and the pinks, yellows, reds and oranges differed almost every day. For painters and writers and for many other people of various backgrounds and interests the valley was an attractive place to live, not only because of its beauty – actually one of my friends refused to be distracted by it and chose to paint in a room without a view -- but also because of its climate and low cost of living in the 50's and 60's. For someone like me who came from the center of New York, the tranquillity of life was entrancing. You could almost live without a clock or watch: certainly Mallorquíns were not as controlled by the time as we were. Today the port is crowded with hotels, souvenir shops, restaurants, bars and apartment houses, but at that time there were only a few fishermen's houses, one or two small hotels and a handful of boats in the bay.

Escha's chalet was on a country lane about a ten-minute walk from the center of the town. In addition, the stop for the trolley which connected Sóller to its port was just up the road. When either of us had a letter to mail, we handed it with a peseta or two to the conductor of the trolley who would drop it off on the mail train to Palma waiting at the station. One afternoon when I was returning from the beach on the trolley and standing on the platform of one of the cars, it gave a lurch and my rolled-up beach mat flew out. At the next stop I got off and walked back to retrieve it, assuming that I would have to wait half an hour for the next trolley. But the conductor saw what had happened and he signalled to the driver to wait until I ran back with my mat. I could just see a New York bus (or trolley, if still in existence) waiting for a passenger in such a situation.

It was spring and I felt on top of the world at the freedom from a daily pressure job. It was wonderful to live in the splendid setting of Sóller, to breathe fresh air, to learn a few words of Spanish every day and gradually to absorb a new culture. The first few weeks Escha had to guide me on where and what to buy and how to get things done in Mallorca. Soon, however, my independent spirit made me shrug off her helping hand as I tried to manage on my own, learning from the many mistakes I made. Of course, I ran into the confusion and embarrassment experienced by many foreigners, caused by the similarity between certain words in English and Spanish but with different meanings, such as, "*constipado*" [having a cold] and "constipated."

(A few parenthetical words about that "independent spirit" I mentioned: I came by that naturally as I was born with no help from anyone except my mother, she and I being the only people in the room. The hospital staff had not believed her when she insisted that my arrival was imminent and that she needed immediate attention. She had been shown into a room and momentarily left alone during which time I had apparently decided that it was time to make my appearance.)

I also had difficulty sometimes in locating a shop or office in Sóller as few of them had identifying signs outside. After all, surely everyone in town knew everyone else.... And there were so many holidays here, far more than in the United States. In addition, if a holiday falls on a Tuesday or a Thursday, many workers take the Monday or Friday off; that is called a *puente* [bridge].

I enjoyed exploring the country lanes – it was so very different from the noisy, dirty streets of the city where I had lived for so long – and I admired the dry stone walls, built without mortar, for which Mallorca, as well as Provence and other Mediterranean areas, is famous. There are many styles of construction, and to this day thousands of kilometres of such walls still exist in agricultural areas, vertical as well as horizontal. The walls had been built and the land behind levelled, providing terraces on which to plant   Stone paved roadways had been laid out with steps for donkeys and man. In some walls there are small holes to permit water to seep out and give people a foothold to climb up. In the mountainous regions there are the remains of snow houses, some of which have been restored, where snow was collected to supply ice year-round. Trails are now well marked for hikers. In recent years there has been great interest shown in preserving the workmanship of the ancestors of present-day Mallorquíns, and there are schools to teach the ancient methods of dry stone construction. Interestingly enough, no historian, archeologist, anthropologist or geographer can date with assurance the origin of these walls or determine the cultural groups which first erected them.

Incidentally, the original town hall dated from 1733 but was obviously inadequate in the twentieth century. Work began on a new structure in the late 60's or early 70's, then stopped dead due to problems with the builder. The huge crane remained towering over the square for years, but finally in 1976 the new town hall was inaugurated with great ceremony.

When I opened my first bank account in Sóller in 1959 at the Hispano Americano, I had to show my passport – you cannot conduct any official business in Spain without showing your passport or residence permit, if you are a foreigner, or your DNI (*Documento nacional de identidad*), if you are a Spaniard – so my account was opened in the name I was known by in the United States, Helen G. Davis. After I had resided here a few years, I gave up the use of Helen G. to become simply Elena Davis. I had never liked the name Helen and the letter "h" is silent in Spanish anyway. I now sign almost all documents here, including checks and even others which show in print my full name, as Elena Davis, and no one has ever objected.

This brings up an unbelievable story involving a foreign name. One of my dear friends was Boris Krakoczi. He is, alas, no longer with us, but many years ago he bought a little house in Fornalutx from a Canadian woman, Clara, who had bought it from a Mallorquín. When Boris died, I helped his grandson, who inherited the house, with various official papers and then sold the house for him. Paul's *escritura* [deed] seemed to take a long time to come through. Two or three times I went to the notary's office to inquire about why it had not yet been registered, and each time there was some reason Finally, however, the notary's assistant explained that the two previous sales had not been registered properly in Palma. The easiest way out of the dilemma was to "skip over" Boris's ownership and indicate in the new document that the grandson had obtained the property directly from Clara (the lack of registration in her name did not seem to matter). As Paul's last name also was Krakoczi, a most unusual name in Spain, probably no one checking the papers would notice that the first names were different. Just to be sure, however, a public notice would be published. So this is how the matter was handled, and the deed came through at last.

Not the least of the advantages of life here was the arrival six days a week of a young woman who did all our housework. Paquita worked two or three hours every day, and we paid her seven pesetas an hour when she began – nowadays the average salary for what she did is approximately one hundred and sixty-eight times as much. By the end of two years her rate had gone up to nine pesetas. She also worked in one of the many textile factories where the employees had morning hours one week and afternoon-evening hours the next, so Paquita alternated her time with us. The factory schedule was hard, particularly in winter, as morning work began at 5 a.m. and finished at 1'30 p.m., and like most work places the factory was unheated. Afternoons went from I p.m. to 9'30 at night. At that time there were fourteen textile factories in Sóller; now they have all disappeared. With the cost of transportation and other factors, they could not compete with the mainland.

Two or three days after we hired Paquita, her mother María, whom we later named the Shrieking Shrew for obvious reasons, came to advise us that her daughter had an illegitimate baby of four months and to explain how at the age of seventeen Paquita had been drugged by a young man, Pep, who then "took advantage of her." She soon realized that she was pregnant but Pep denied responsibility. At a meeting in a lawyer's office before the birth of the baby, he said that he was not the father but was willing to marry Paquita. Her father said to her, "You need not marry him if you do not want to," and she did not. Incidentally, as the child grew up he was the spitting image of Pep who, so far as I know, never did acknowledge the relationship.

While Paquita was still living at home, life was not easy for her. In the social ambience of that time the child was not discriminated against but she was. One day it was obvious she was very unhappy as she wanted to see the Saturday night American movie, *"Mas allá de Mombassa"* ["Beyond Mombassa"]. Her brothers did not want to take her with them, naturally she had no boy friend, and it was unthinkable that she go out at night alone. So Escha and I invited her to go with us. I still remember the ridiculous scenes in the film in which the heroine remained immaculate with makeup and hair in perfect condition after some terrifying episodes in darkest Africa. But Paquita was in heaven.

Paquita continued to live at home for a few years until she was offered an opportunity to work in Paris in a private home. She left the child with her parents who encouraged him to accept them as his parents. After she was established in

Paris she came back for the child and had him with her for a year or so, but that arrangement did not work out and the child returned to his grandparents who brought him up. Eventually Paquita married a Frenchman and made a new life for herself in his country.

Incidentally, her father Pablo walked the railroad tracks every day from Sóller to Bunyola, some thirteen kilometers, to check the ties. He rode back on a small electric car. His highest salary at the end of his working days was thirteen thousand pesetas monthly. Later his older son became the chef of a five-star hotel on the mainland and earned five times as much. But Pablo enjoyed his life; he was a thoughtful man and had many serious discussions with Escha on life, politics and other subjects. (Unfortunately my knowledge of Spanish then was too limited for me to take much part in those conversations.) In his spare time Pablo made fine wrought iron lamps and tables, some of which I have in my house.

A neighbor of theirs had an unfortunate background. Ana was brought up by a couple who were not her parents. She was not ill-treated but as they had very limited means, she received only a minimal education and at age twelve had to begin to work as a house cleaner. She had no information about her father but eventually learned that her mother was a member of an upper class family in another area. The desire to meet her grew until she could not fight it any longer. Now a grown woman, she presented herself at her mother's house without having given any notice of her intentions. The servant who opened the door to Ana told her she could not come in as her *señora* was not well; but she more or less forced her way in, went upstairs and found her mother. She said to her, "I wanted only to look at the face of the woman who gave birth to me and then deserted me" I did not learn what the mother replied, but Ana told me that she had left immediately and had never laid eyes on her mother again, nor did she wish to.

My first few months I was not too active as I had been overworking in New York for many years, but eventually I settled into a regime under which five afternoons a week I studied Spanish by myself for two hours; good teaching was hard to come by as I had learned on my two earlier visits when I had taken Spanish lessons. I liked the teacher personally with whom I had studied, but the book she used was designed to teach French to Spanish speakers – not much help to me. Meanwhile because I did not know whether I could make a living here, I sent to California for two tomes on real estate law with the idea that if matters did not work out financially for me in Mallorca, I could return to the United States and enter a new field of occupation there. I put in two hours of study daily in this area also. It is interesting that I considered work as a real estate agent as a possibility inasmuch as I fell into that occupation in Mallorca almost by accident a little later on.

In 1960 a Canadian friend and I investigated the possibility of initiating a discount shopping service for tourists. We interviewed many store proprietors and managers in Palma who evidenced interest in such a plan. But when we looked into all the legal and tax requirements, we realized that the project was not viable because of all the red tape and contradictory regulations. The idea was good and later on others were able to establish services of this type when the authorities recognized how important to the local economy spending by foreign visitors could be, and the rules were eased.

At the time I regretted that we could not proceed with our project, but on the other hand, I should have had to commute to Palma five or six days of the week by train. If we had gone on with the idea, there would have been no Sóller English Lending Library, nor would I have developed a property management business. In fact, my whole life here would have been different.

Villa Rua was located in a very damp part of the valley, so the house was not very comfortable during part of the year, even with the fireplaces as they were small ones. We allowed ourselves one hot bath a week, and for that we lighted the *cocina económica,* the wood-burning stove in the kitchen, some hours beforehand. Of course, that day we also cooked on it; anything roasted in an *económica* has a wonderful flavor.

When Escha first took over Villa Rua she cooked on two small *petroleo* stoves. The fuel smelled and she had to clean the wicks daily, a very messy job. It wasn't practical every day to light the *económica* and keep it going just for herself. Then in 1957 she discovered a new type of stove, a Firpe, which was powered by electricity that changed a special liquid into gas. She had this installed in time for my visit that year, and it certainly made food preparation much easier. There was one drawback, however: At times the supply of electrical current was cut, generally at noon or 1 p.m. when we were preparing lunch, our principal meal of the day. We never knew how long the cut would last; and if the time dragged on without electricity, we had to decide whether to wait a bit longer or start up the *económica* which would need almost an hour to heat up enough to continue cooking. Electricity first came to Sóller in

1908 and, oddly enough, the company was called El Gas until the first of 2005 as it had supplied that fuel years before. (The first village on the island to have electrical current was Alaró, installed in 1901. A historical note in a newspaper pointed out that the first street oil lamps in Palma appeared in 1803. In 1812 one thousand lamps were installed but were lit only from September to May except when there was a full moon!)

Although we had no luxury foods, we ate chicken, lamb and pork, all of which were, and still are, excellent here. And, of course, fresh fish. Good beef was scarce. Most of our cooking pots were made of unglazed earthenware. When we bought a new *olla* or *greixonera*, we treated it with oil, garlic and tomato which we cooked in it for some hours to close the pores and make it watertight. Nowadays that procedure is not necessary as the pots have already been glazed. Incidentally, a friend gave us an English pressure cooker as she was afraid of it, and it is still in use in my house today, some forty-six years later.

The evening meal for the local people could be boring as in many modest homes the main dish every night was *sopes mallorquines*. This almost dry soup can be delicious if made with a variety of vegetables and some meat as well as the cut-thin saltless brown bread; this used to be stale bread left over from once-a-week home baking, but eventually it became available finely sliced at bakeries. Frequently for reasons of economy, the dish consisted only of the bread in a soup which was made of water, garlic, onions, olive oil and cabbage. At least two of my students said the equivalent of, "If I never eat it again it will be too soon." Nonetheless, their healthful diet plus the outdoor physical life led by many Mallorquíns produced a great number of healthy ninety-year-olds, and centenarians are not unusual.

As for olive oil, they consumed large quantities. A student of mine, an eighteen-year-old, once told me that he, his parents and sister used two liters a week in their food! And, of course, *pa amb oli* [bread with oil] is a typical snack here. Tomás Graves actually wrote and published a book devoted to this dish, called in English, not surprisingly, "Bread & Oil," though I believe he wrote it originally in Mallorquín. The olive tree goes back to at least 4,000 B.C., and there are approximately 800,000,000 of them in the world. Some of the best olive oil produced in Spain comes from Mallorca. Many of the women in Sóller and the neighboring village of Fornalutx who did not work in the textile factories or elsewhere used to pick olives in the fall and winter, a backbreaking job as the ripe olives were on the ground. You still see some women going off with their pails but nowadays, at least, they all wear slacks to protect themselves from the damp earth.

Even in winter when the water rushing down from the mountains was icy cold, the women washed their clothes outdoors in the public laundry, their houses not being supplied with running water. Some of the local women cooked outdoors on charcoal, and the doors to their houses were open as they went back and forth. Well I remember two winter meals as a guest in neighbors' houses when I wore a coat at the table. There was a big fireplace but much of the warmth seemed to go up the chimney, and there was no other form of heat in the house. Our hosts did not seem to feel the cold. In addition, I was taken aback when the husband put the big round bread under the armpit of his shirt and with his working knife cut off a thick slice and handed it to me. In fact, one of the children might have gone to the bakery to buy the loaf, and it could have been handed it to him unwrapped. He might even have used it as a ball to play with a friend! Gradually, however, the bakeries began to wrap the loaf in a small piece of paper.

In 1959 or 1960 we had an "Alaska" stove made in which we burned huge chunks of olive root which were available then. An Englishman here claimed to have invented this type of heater in Alaska; it was made of round galvanized iron with a metal tube which rose through the house and out of the roof. We called it the monster because it seemed to consume quite a lot of wood. This was certainly not central heating, but it gave some warmth to the house and kept down the humidity. In addition, on the six bathless nights of the week in cold weather we hung two pails of water on the railing around the stove to have hot water with which to wash. The bathroom temperature did not encourage us to linger long over our ablutions. Generally we washed dishes in cold water, which shocked me at first, but I soon got used to it.

In addition to factories and other such buildings having no heat, the same was true of schools; so the children used to warm stones, wrap newspapers around them and hold them to keep their hands warm. Before leaving the house in the morning, the children had a *café con leche* (with probably more milk than coffee) and then ate their breakfast on the way to school – a roll or hunk of bread with a piece of chocolate or *sobrasada,* the Mallorquín sausage made of finely minced pork, salt and paprika. (Almost 2,700 tons of *sobrasada* are made annually, a small proportion of it from the Mallorquin black pig which is considered to produce the best.)

Like all our neighbors we had no refrigerator. On my first two visits here we kept the butter and milk (the latter was delivered daily by the milk woman or her daughter, unpasteurized, so we boiled it – it is amazing how quickly milk boils over when your back is turned) in a pail down the well in the kitchen. If we bought meat a day in advance of cooking it, we covered it with a film of oil or, if pork, with salt and put it into the cool cupboard in the kitchen under the stairway. Toward the end of the 50's Escha had bought an ice chest, and from then on every morning a little boy from the neighborhood delivered a piece of ice. The trouble was we never knew whether we'd find it melting on the doorstep when we got up or would have to wait until 10 or 11 a.m. for it. For this service the youngster was paid one or two pesetas daily.

One summer in the early 60's when Judith and family were visiting, I went to get the *bifsteks* from the chest and was shocked to see them covered with hundreds of small crawling ants. My immediate feeling was to throw the meat away, but Escha assured me that after the ants had been washed away, the steaks were perfectly safe. We did eat them, I with slightly long teeth, but no one suffered any after-effects.

Ants could be a nuisance in other ways. The same year they invaded the icebox I had them in my clothes on the shelves and in my bed until I put ant powder around each leg (not mine, I hasten to add), but some years we saw barely half a dozen in the house. As for other potentially unpleasant creatures, while there are some snakes on the island, none is poisonous. During all the time I have lived here I have seen only two or three, one of which was stretched out dead on the floor when I came home one day; it measured about eighteen inches. My cat was sitting beside it with what I took to be a very satisfied look on her face. We do have scorpions and spiders, of course, but they are not a problem. I was amused to hear a couple of years ago of an English couple who had cemented over all of their garden after the wife saw a snake under a bush.

I had to give up my prejudices and fears in many areas. One morning on entering the kitchen, we could scarcely walk as the floor was covered with slugs which had come up from the sink drainpipe. They were really nasty-looking and neither of us wanted to touch them, but we managed to get rid of the horrors. After that the drainpipe was kept tightly plugged.

There were many things that were different to those I was accustomed to, perhaps not very important, but which I had to accommodate myself to as, for example, calendars. Spanish ones show Monday as the first day of the week; in America it is Sunday. Here we use a Centigrade thermometer; in the United States, a Fahrenheit. In Spain and many other countries buildings of a number of floors have the ground floor, then the first, the second, and so on whereas in the U.S. the ground floor is called the first; the next one, the second, et cetera.

Escha's mattress was made of wool which was fine in winter but not so comfortable in summer. Mine, though, was made of *cle* (or *cli*), fibers from the heart of the palm tree. Pep Matalassser [Pepe the Mattressman] of the Street of Seven Houses came every year to treat the mattress. He opened the cotton cover, took out the contents in small bunches and very skillfully beat each with two special sticks, then stuffed it all back and sewed up the cover. At first, the mattress was wonderful; but gradually the material sank down in the middle. After two or three years of using this mattress I began to develop back trouble so finally bought a modern one. Some country

38

people of limited means, at least on the mainland, used leaves from corn cobs as stuffing for mattresses.

I had brought with me an electric blanket which here required the use of a transformer. This was something I'd never employed in the United States or even heard of. The model available in Sóller was big and heavy, and unfortunately it did not work or, at least, the blanket did not. The thick, heavy blankets on my bed did not keep me comfortable on cold nights, so I threw my American winter coat (which in fifty years I never wore in Spain and finally gave away) on top which helped. Not until a couple of years later did a visitor from the United States play with the transformer and get it to function. What pleasure then to get into a warm bed in winter when the house temperature was low. I have to add that many years afterwards I awoke one morning to find a corner of the blanket burned away – a lucky escape for me.

Mosquito nets over the beds were a necessity for most people. They were made of an old umbrella frame and some eighteen meters of netting. During my first years on the island I was not bothered much by bites, but gradually I lost my immunity. Still, once I moved to Fornalutx in 1971 I never needed a net again. By then, of course, there were many kinds of anti-mosquito products on sale here. (Authorities disagree on the origin of the name Fornalutx; there have actually been ten different forms of the name during its existence.)

In contrast to our life today, there was no crime to speak of. Windows and doors were left open or unlocked. In fact, when you went out, you left your key in the lock outside. *"Mi casa es su casa."* ["My house is your house."] Life which had been so hard for the Mallorquíns during and for many years after the

Civil War [the "*Movimiento*"] was gradually improving. The men sang as they worked in the fields, in quarter-tone Arabic music. Mothers when they went shopping or worked in nearby houses could leave their seven- or eight-year-old girls or boys in charge of infants, who seemed to enjoy their responsibility. Traffic generally presented no danger because there were so few cars, and motorcycles and motorbikes were fairly scarce.

An oddity about the lack of traffic on the streets of Sóller: On Sunday or holiday evenings you often saw a family walking home from the square in the dusk or dark, without a flashlight, with mother, father and three or four or more children side by side, with the smallest one out in the middle of the street. There was little likelihood then of a fast car coming up from behind, but this custom persisted until cars became more numerous. If anyone had been hit, it would have been the infant.

Crime certainly exists today so it was amazing one day a year or so ago to see the Queen of Spain accompanied by only her daughter, her son-in-law and their children on the open trolley from the Sóller station to the port where they lunched and spent the day. It was a private visit to the valley, and there were no guards visible. King Juan Carlos before ascending to the throne came once or twice to lunch in the port at one of our best seafood restaurants; and as King he also lunched there once, the owner having been given two hours' notice. Someone in his party paid the bill, but he left the tip and also went into the kitchen to compliment the cook.

Mallorquíns were accustomed to walking everywhere, and, in fact, some Sollerenses who worked in the port about four kilometres away walked there and back twice a day if they did not own bicycles. We generally did a lot of walking also except that we sometimes took the trolley to the port (the fare which was nine-tenths of a peseta is now five hundred and fifty-five times as much) or only very occasionally a taxi. In winter when we went on foot to a party, we women usually carried our "good" shoes with us and changed at our hosts' house.

Motorbikes and motorcycles became popular in the 50's and 60's. A man I knew was the first one on his street to buy a Vespa 125 in the early 50's. Rather daringly, he and his fourteen-year-old son toured Spain for three weeks.

I bought a Mobylette in the 60's for the equivalent of about $175 and was only the second woman in Sóller to ride a motorbike. The first was an American friend of mine who came here from time to time. On one of my trips to London later on I purchased a helmet as they had none small enough for me here, carrying it back over my arm, which brought a smile to the faces of some of the passengers on the airplane. Helmets were not compulsory then – a fact that resulted in tragedy for some families as at least four young men whom I knew were injured or killed in motorbike accidents. None was wearing a helmet. I had a permit to run my Mobylette but no test had been required to obtain it. It seemed curious to me, but after I got my Spanish driving license and had my first car, a civil guard came to my house one day to pick up this permit which he said I no longer needed.

It took me a little while to feel completely comfortable on my two-wheeler, but soon I was whizzing back and forth to Palma over the mountains some thirty kilometers away – no tunnel then. I also took a few days off and made a tour around the island.

There were not many private cars in Sóller in the early 50's; it was still very much of a luxury item. There was a vehicle, the Isocarro, which ran on three wheels, but this was used chiefly for transporting goods and not passengers. The Isetta had two rear wheels and two small centered front ones. It was known as *El Huevo* [The Egg] because of its shape; you got into the car from the front. There was also a small car called the David. When Escha arrived in 1952 some of the cars were run on almond shells which were converted into fuel.

The Biscuter came on the market in 1953. It was designed by a Frenchman, Gabriel Voisin. Until then only the well-to-do here could afford to buy cars, but he had a dream to produce an economic vehicle, one with comfortable space for two or three people which was able to reach an average speed of sixty kilometers an hour. Its maximum speed was seventy kilometers. The Biscuter was produced in Barcelona from 1953 to 1959, and a total of twelve to fourteen thousand were fabricated. Its initial price was twenty-five thousand pesetas. The demise of the Biscuter was due to competition; in 1959, for example, the price had risen to almost sixty thousand pesetas whereas you could buy a superior car, the Seat, for just ten thousand more.

Don Jorge, the lawyer, was one of the first people in Sóller to buy a Biscuter. He was the person most of the British turned to for help when they bought a property here. He was a charming gentleman but, alas, not the most efficient of lawyers. Friends of mine waited almost eight years for him to produce the deed to their finca though the delay was not all his fault. In his favor, you might think, was the fact that he was most lax in billing people for his services, as his widow sadly acknowledged when

I mentioned it to her after his death the day I went to pay my respects.

The *taxistas* usually had Dodges, some of which were thirty years old, into which they could pack many passengers. There was no bus service between Sóller and Fornalutx, two and a half kilometers away, so you went on foot or took a private taxi or the "taxi-bus", a big Dodge, which twice a day met the train from Palma and took the mail up to the village. Some years ago bus service was established between the two communities, but it was cancelled after only one day. Last year a new service was begun connecting Sóller, the nearby hamlet of Biniaraix and Fornalutx, but Biniaraix has been dropped from the route.

When I returned to the United States the first time in 1962, my brother met me at the airport and drove me to his home. On the highway something bothered me, but it was a while before I realized what it was: The road was full of women drivers. This was in stark contrast to the situation in Sóller where there might have been one or two, but there was certainly none in Fornalutx.

It could be difficult to get a definite answer on a legal regulation. For example, my friend Betty had a British-plated car, a Triumph, which she brought over to Mallorca to use on her long visits. We went to see the Aduana [Customs Office] to clarify her position because she had been told that the car would have to be sealed if it (or was it she?) were here for more than six months. The official was pleasant but was not sure himself, so he escorted us to see the director. He, too, was most affable but refused to commit himself, saying the regulations were confusing and contradictory. He smiled at us apologetically. And that's where the matter lay.

If you sell your car here, you must be sure that the buyer follows through with the registration process and pays the fees. If not, the car remains legally in your name, you are responsible for any accident that may occur and, in addition, for the annual road tax. Two or three of my friends have been stuck with considerable amounts to pay years after selling as taxes and fines accumulated, the buyers of their cars not having completed the paper work or paid what they owed. And I had a problem when I sold my second Seat 600 because the buyer delayed registering the car and in that period when the car was still in my name, he got a traffic ticket which he did not pay. It took a bit of effort on my part to rid myself of the legal responsibility for it.

A note about present-day car ownership: In 2003 in the Balearics there were six hundred and four vehicles per one thousand inhabitants, the highest ratio in all of Spain. (The figure for Madrid was five hundred and thirty.) But at a meeting in Palma in October, 2004, it was stated that there were nine hundred and fifty motorized vehicles per thousand - of course, this figure includes trucks, tractors, motorcycles, et cetera. In addition, there are thirty thousand cars for hire. The authorities are extremely concerned about the number of road deaths on the islands, almost seventy   during the first eight months of 2005. On the first of July, 2006, the point system was put into effect under which a driver loses points for driving infractions. Each of us began with twelve points and if a driver loses all of them, he may not legally drive. It is complicated and costly to get some of them back. And so far though some people seem to be driving more carefully, accidents continue at almost the same rate as before.

Regarding Mallorquin drivers, they may know how to drive a car but seem not to know about the courtesy of the road, and more and more of them now drive carelessly, even recklessly. The motorcyclists are the worst, and I have been the victim in two unpleasant accidents. In one case two off-duty Palma policemen were racing up the "American" road, which they do Saturday nights, and the younger one crashed into my car. The other who had gone ahead did not see the accident but later claimed he was a witness and would testify against me. I was sued and would surely have lost the case, being a foreign woman in my 80's and without a witness on my side. Fortunately, my insurance company settled the afternoon of the day before I was scheduled to appear in court, the lawyer having told me I would have otherwise lost my license.

Nonetheless, the local drivers are great in one way as when a driver stops to chat with someone in the street, sometimes for quite a long time, no one behind ever honks. Everyone sits quietly in her/his car and waits patiently for the first driver to move on.

Some of my friends who had cars applied for Spanish driver's licenses while it was still easy to obtain if you had a license from another country. Although I did not own a car I thought it advisable to get one, just in case. I still had my American license, but that would not be valid for a resident here. (My New York State license dated back to when I was sixteen. At that time – and this may still be true – junior licenses were available to youngsters that age. They were limited to journeys "to and fro" school and to errands for one's parents.)

All I had to do here was pass the practical test but not the written part. I signed up for one lesson with the Darder agency in

Palma so I could learn of any requirement that was different from the rules with which I was familiar in New York. That proved to be a good idea as there were two. On the day of the test, I rode my Mobylette to the grounds in Palma and parked it. The agency supplied the Seat 600 which I was to use for the examination. Even if I had owned a car I would not have been permitted to use it. (This regulation was hard on Carla, a close friend of mine, who was almost six feet tall, and the 600 scarcely allowed room for her legs and feet.) Another applicant, a Spaniard, sat in the back with the Darder representative, and the examiner was next to me. I am very short so I moved my seat forward and with exaggerated motions adjusted the two mirrors, the agency having told me that this was most important. The test was not difficult. When the examiner said I was finished, he told me and the Spaniard to exchange positions. The minute he started off I knew he had failed as though taller than I (well, everyone is), he did not adjust his seat or the mirrors and had to lean forward awkwardly to use them.

I had had no conversation with the examiner; but when the car drew up at the end of the man's test, I pointed to my Mobylette and said, "That's my car." He replied in astonishment, "You drove over the mountain from Sóller on that?" and of course I said yes. *"Muy valiente."* he replied.

The following day I called the agency to get the expected news that I had passed and was dumbfounded to be told that I had failed. They could not give me the reason as they said the examiner reported only the names of the successful candidates. During two weeks until the next examination I was extremely upset wondering what I had done wrong. No one I knew had failed. Even a woman who did not know how to back up (literally) had passed!

When I showed up for the second time the examiner recognized me, thanks to my Mobylette, and was surprised to see me. He said that certainly I had passed, that I had done very well. In that case, why had the agency told me that I had not? He had the grace to look a bit uncomfortable. It seems that he had misplaced my card and so had not at first reported my passing the test. He assured me, however, that later he had done so. The agency said that he had not, but I did get my license, so *Todo va bien que acaba bien.* [All's well than ends well.]

I finally bought a secondhand, or possibly thirdhand, Seat 600 in 1971 and exchanged it for another slightly better one a few years later. The day after I became the owner of the first one, I decided to practice a bit as I had never driven in Mallorca. I took the car up a narrow mountain road with a stream on the right and then tried to turn around. After the first maneuver to the left, I realized that I did not know how to get into reverse, the gear shift being different from any that I knew. Fortunately, the car was on an incline so I let it roll back and then continued up the road to a place where I could turn. As soon as I got back to my starting point, though I was embarrassed to do so, I asked the first driver I met and he showed me how to find reverse gear.

At different times I took my little Seat over to the mainland to tour the country. Once when I was on a country road, the motor began to smoke. I had no water with me but managed to scoop some dirty liquid up from a stream nearby for the radiator, so I could limp along to the next town where the garage mechanic told me that the radiator that had been put into the car by the jack-of-all-trades in my village when he had repaired it a short while before was not a Seat model. Although my funds were limited, I had no choice but to have a new radiator installed.

One afternoon in the 50's when we had an invitation from friends in Fornalutx, we went up to the railroad station and got into the waiting taxi-bus. When the train disgorged its passengers, there were twelve human beings, including the driver and two babies, who tried to squeeze into the car. Some of these people were regulars, so the driver told us we should have to get out. Escha said no, we were legitimate passengers; and even though there were some black looks, she stuck to her guns. All twelve of us, therefore, started off sardined into the taxi. Fortunately, we dropped off two or three people on the way. The cost of this trip was five pesetas. When Jaume of Fornalutx retired (he was the first person in the village to own a car), his son Benet took the service on until the midi-80's when it was discontinued as by then many people had their own cars, and there were plenty of taxis. The charge now for the run by taxi between Sóller and Fornalutx is fifteen times as much as it was in 1990.

The station, by the way, had been a fortified building known as Can Mayol, and was rebuilt in 1911-12 in time for the inauguration of the railroad, the only one privately owned in Spain, on the 16th of April, 1912. The trolley line to the port entered service a year later. The train originally ran with steam engines which later were replaced by electric motors. The great-grandson of the founder of the railroad, both called Jeroni Estades, studied English with me in the 60's.

Fornalutx was one of the most beautiful and unspoiled villages in Spain and is still well preserved although now the amount of new construction is almost unbelievable and, if it continues, will surely detract from its charm. What helps to maintain the attractiveness of the place is the ruling that all exteriors must be of natural stone. And there are still kilometres of dry stone walls in the village and surrounding areas. Some of the house eaves still have what are claimed to be Moorish tiles. Fornalutx has been awarded prizes a number of times for its appearance by organisations, such as the Mallorquín Tourist Board and the General Secretary for Tourism.

When I came here in the 50's the first time, I learned that many of the older residents of the village had never been to Palma, and there may have been some who had never even visited Sóller, a few kilometers away. There were old people who believed in witches – and I am sure that some still do -- and we heard that if a virgin wanted her *novio* [boy friend] to propose to her, all she had to do was put a drop of her menstrual blood in his drink, presumably when he was not looking.

The mountain road over the *Coll* between Sóller and the plain leading to Palma was scenic but its many narrow turns made it dangerous. Those long Dodges used as taxis had to maneuver quite a bit to get around the worst of the curves which have long since been widened. The *taxistas* had the habit of stopping at the little bar at the top on their way back from the airport to have a *copa* or *copita* (little drink) which was generally a *coñac*. The first time or so that this happened, I was a bit uneasy at the thought of all those turns still to come, but the drink never seemed to affect the driver adversely. This road is now not used very much except by tourists who have been told about its magnificent scenery as the long-discussed tunnel through the mountain opened on February 19, 1997, and most traffic to and from Palma takes advantage of it though the toll is quite pricey for non-residents. As a result of this lack of traffic and subsequent diminution in his business, the owner of the little bar where we used to stop near the top committed suicide. At least, they say that was his reason.

The tunnel had been under discussion for years. A plan had been drawn up under which a tunnel would be built and completed by 1973, but nothing came of this. Then in 1975 the national minister for public works was on the island and said that not only would a tunnel be very expensive but also that it was "not viable." Obviously, later on other people had different ideas.

While the tunnel was being built, I vowed never to use it and earlier had even signed a petition against the construction of it; like many other people here I thought Sóller's already crowded streets would be overrun by visitors, and it would become a bedroom community for people who worked in Palma. The day after its inauguration, however, I was forced to go through it in order to catch a plane, my departure from the house having been delayed by a loquacious caller who would not let me off the phone. Now I use the tunnel at least ten or fifteen times a month (one September I actually went through it ten times in the same number of days), and the tolls I, as a resident, pay are now reimbursed by the government a couple of months later.

Another project which was being considered in the 60's but took years to be carried out was the Paseo Marítimo in Palma, the avenue along the bay which separates the sea from the Cathedral, La Lonja and many other buildings. The historian

Luis Ripoll wrote in distress in 1965, "The old city, birthplace of navigators, capital of the island, belongs to the sea; its walls have always been lapped by the sea. Now the sea is two hundred metres away. It is a serious cause for disgust." Today with its steady stream of traffic it seems hard to believe that once it was covered by the Mediterranean.

In 1960 or 1961 Escha bought a secondhand piano in Palma and eagerly awaited its delivery so that her accompanist and she could practice at home. Finally the truck arrived with only the driver and one other man and with no special equipment or dolly. They looked around and hailed two men working in a field who ambled over. After a lengthy discussion and much to-ing and fro-ing, the four men manhandled the piano on to the ground and then carried it into the house with Escha anxiously looking on. They all had earned and accepted the *copa* she offered each man, as well as the generous tip. Had there been no men working nearby to give a hand, I suppose the piano would still be on the truck.

One Mallorquín custom, taken up by most of the foreigners, was that of kissing each other on both cheeks when meeting. This was somewhat disturbing to me as I came from a family which was not demonstrative, and in New York I did not move in circles in which people greeted each other by kissing and calling the other person, "Darling." So at first I was a bit hesitant but soon found that I liked the warmth of the greeting. Eventually it amused me to see some of the more reserved English residents looking uncomfortable when being kissed by someone who was not an intimate. It also pleased me that everyone greeted every passerby with a *"bon día"* or *"bones tardes*". The atmosphere was certainly different from my area in New York where I had lived for so many years.

Mallorquíns often asked personal questions, such as, "How old are you?" and "How much rent do you pay?" And Escha, who was older than I but not that much, would have been offended if she had known that a few times someone referred to her as my mother, fortunately not in her presence. When I came to live here, I was one of the youngest of the so-called foreign colony; now I am almost the oldest.

There were frequent village and family fiestas, and we were sometimes invited to the latter which was a great privilege because most Spaniards at that time might meet a friend in a café or restaurant but seldom, if the person was not an intimate, in his own home.. On the night of the sixteenth of January there was an enormous bonfire in each neighborhood to celebrate Saint Antonio. The men and boys spent days beforehand gathering huge tree trunks, and that night the local people came together round the fire, one or two with a *ximbomba*, a musical "instrument" made from a gourd, to play and sing for hours. The verses they sang, often improvised, were slightly off color or made fun of the government or the Guardia Civil – and this was during Franco's day. You brought your own refreshments and often your own chair. The fire was so hot that your front was burning while your backside began to freeze as the hours passed. The custom of the fires for Saint Antonio continues in some places, but it has lost much of its neighbourhood intimacy though the town hall in Fornalutx annually arranges a splendid fire and offers free refreshments to one and all.

Every village and town has an annual fiesta on its saint's

day; and while they differ in many details, all of them include lots of noise-making and fireworks. In my village they still run a "bull;" I put quotation marks around the word because it is only a half-grown (or even younger) animal. Spanish law now prohibits the inclusion of animals in local fiestas unless the tradition is one hundred or more years old. Only one or two other villages on Mallorca are thus permitted to have a bull run, known as a *carrebou*. Fortunately, thanks to the watchfulness of the animal shelters and protests by others, the animals may be terrified half to death but are now not actually tortured. I keep my windows and front door locked the night before and the morning of the bullrun; and if possible, I spend the time somewhere else.

Long before I came to Spain I had, of course, heard about bullfighting – and I had certainly read my Hemingway. But I did not honestly know much about the subject, except that I was against it. I am still. I never wanted to see a bullfight and went only once many years ago when a friend insisted that it was shameful to be prejudiced against something that I had never witnessed. I had bad luck that day. There was a "*rejoneador*" [bullfighter mounted on horseback], and the bull gored the horse in the stomach or intestines. The horse made no sound – it could not, I was told, as its vocal chords had previously been cut. They came and put the poor horse to death, it was dragged away – and the show went on. I stayed for the other five fights, hoping to see one of the "*toreadores*" get what I felt would be his just deserts, but they all escaped unhurt. My sympathies are always with the animals. It is obvious –- and I admit to this –- that I do not understand the Spaniard's feelings about bullfights.

Bullfighting has declined seriously in popularity during the years. Sunday afternoons everyone used to be glued to the radio before TV came to the island. When the cafés began to install TV, the men went there to watch it. Nowadays, except for a hard core of *aficionados*, it is usually *futbol* (soccer to Americans) which draws the viewers.

During our village fiesta which lasts four or five days there is a special event in our plaza, Homage to the Elderly, when each resident of 70 or more years (except one American woman who refuses to take part) is honored. Each such person is called up, accompanied by a young "sponsor", to be congratulated and kissed by the local authorities and presented with various gifts, the oldest one first, then one by one down to the youngest There were fifteen, twenty or more oldies ahead of me when I was first included in the ceremony. Now I am fifth on the list and our oldest is a fully *compos mentis* ninety-nine-year-old. People here live to a good age. A year or so ago our oldest died a few weeks after reaching his one hundredth birthday. And that age is not unusual in the valley. In fact, one very well dressed Mallorquín walks through Sóller every day for an hour, and he is 101 years old. When I saw him the other day and stopped to chat, I inquired smilingly, "How old are you, *señor*?" And he replied in the same spirit, "Twelve and a half."

The holiday not celebrated was a person's birthday. The important day was her/his saint's day. I had a student who came one day when it happened to be her tenth birthday, and of course I congratulated her. Later that day when I saw her mother and remarked on the birthday, she looked surprised and after a few seconds said, "Oh, yes, so it is." I found it had to believe that a mother would not remember her little girl's date of birth.

At 6 p.m. every day Escha and I stopped whatever we each had been doing and met on the upstairs terrace with its fabulous view of the fruit trees stretching across the valley and the mountains behind to enjoy our "witch's brew", almonds and olives. Escha was the witch (she had red hair and green eyes), and her drink was an exceptionally mild martini so we could have a number of them without actually overdoing on the alcohol. The gin we bought *a granel*, i.e., we took an empty bottle or two to the *bodega* [wine shop] where they sold two or three types of gin loose and bought a liter or so. We had to be careful not to take the perfumed gin on offer. They also sold about five qualities of brandy, and you were encouraged to taste the contents of each barrel before making a selection. After imbibing a goodly sample of each, you really did not care which you bought. We always kept a bottle in the house as if someone delivered a big object or did some work for you, you offered a drink as Escha had done when the men delivered the piano, and the usual prompt reply was, *"Venga."* ["Let's have it."].

Wine and vermouth were also sold *a granel*. We sometimes bought sixteen liters at a time, thirty-six pesetas per liter for gin and twenty-six pesetas for vermouth. (By February, 1965, Vermut Cinzano *seco* [dry] had gone up to thirty.) At the grocer's, too, you could buy powdered cinnamon, peppercorns, coffee ground or in beans, spices, tinned biscuits and many other products in as small or large quantity as you wished, all then skillfully wrapped in a bit of paper, sometimes newspaper, and twisted at each end. The empty biscuit tins were for sale, and they came in very useful for storing different kinds of food after we treated the interior with aluminum paint to prevent rust. At the hardware shops to this day you can buy nails, screws and other such items by the piece or by weight .

Almost no one I knew drank or served whiskey as it was imported and therefore very expensive though there were a couple of Spanish makes, but no comparison with the Scottish product. One winter evening a Mallorquín couple invited Escha and me to come after dinner. The host opened a a bottle of good Scotch and we sat chatting and drinking in comfort as they had installed central heating, a system which used almond shells as fuel. When the bottle was finished, he offered us a final drink but of Spanish whiskey. By this time, as I was unaccustomed to drinking anything so strong, it tasted just as good as the earlier bottle. Escha and I walked home in a happy mood.

The mention of whiskey brings to mind an amusing story: The father of a student of mine was the manager of one of Sóller's banks. One day he asked if he could come to see me with an associate, a lawyer, with a financial document in English for which he wanted a translation. When I saw it, I knew that I was in over my head as my Spanish was still not much better than rudimentary, and the document pertained to an investment in the United States. Nevertheless, as they both knew some English and I had a good English-Spanish dictionary, they obtained sufficient information for their purposes. The bank man then asked me what my fee was, but somewhat embarrassed I told him, "nothing." He asked me if I drank whiskey and I answered affirmatively – I hope not too enthusiastically. He said he would send me a bottle. The days and weeks passed but no whiskey and I forgot about the episode. When I happened to meet him months later in the street, he assured me that he had not forgotten.

Again, nothing until a long time afterwards when a messenger delivered a package to me, and in it was a very fine bottle of the long-promised drink. I thoroughly enjoyed it, even if I had had to wait eighteen months for it.

Occasionally we went to Palma on the train, second class usually, though the temptation of the upholstered armchairs in first class sometimes made us forget that our funds were limited. (Alas, today there is only one class on the train, and the armchairs are gone.) The picturesque journey takes fifty minutes, passes through numerous tunnels and ought not to be missed by any visitor. There has been more than one film made about the *tren de Sóller.*

Some residents had to commute to Palma every day to get to work or to school, taking the early train which was not too convenient, but the second one got them to their destination too late. A whistle which could be heard far from the station signaled the departure of the train supposedly in five minutes. It was purposely four minutes too fast, however; but everyone knew this, so instead of rushing to catch the train, the stragglers took their time. Still, they all had to be on board at the scheduled hour of leaving as the train always departed on the dot. Alas, the whistle signal was discontinued many years ago.

To do our errands we walked all over Palma or took the trolley-bus which I loved. It went as far as El Terreno, then almost the outskirts of the city. (They were taken out of service in 1959 when buses took over.) We often allowed ourselves a stop at a *bodega* for a glass of wine and a "*variada,*" a plate of assorted *"tapas"* [tidbits or appetizers]. The *bodega* is still there with same proprietor but today the cost would be about forty times higher. Occasionally we had lunch at the restaurant Yate Ritz, famous for its three-course very reasonable meal, which closed its doors recently.

There were occasional recitals and concerts in Palma; and after the Auditorium opened in 1969, we were able to enjoy performances by splendid soloists, orchestras and opera companies from many countries. Attendance at a performance meant, however, that we had to use taxis as the Sóller train did not run that late. Years later, when I owned a car, I was driving some friends home from a concert when my little Seat gave up the ghost. It was after midnight, there was almost no traffic on the road and mobile phones did not exist; so I started to walk back where I hoped to find a public phone in order to call RACE, the automobile club. To my delight I found a taxi returning to the city. He took us to Sóller and dropped us off at our various destinations there and in Fornalutx and asked for only a modest amount though he was entitled to more at that hour. Two or three times men have very kindly changed a tire for me when I had a blowout on the road, and though I tried, there was no way I could pay them.

Pollensa had an outstanding annual music festival, initiated in 1962, which is still going strong, where some of the world's best artists have performed. Sometimes before any of us owned a car a group went over the mountain to Pollensa by taxi. Once I went on my Mobylette and stayed overnight at a *hostal* there with four of us squeezed into one room as I did not relish the idea of coming back on my motorbike on that road late at night. For some years there have also been regular recitals and concerts of high quality in neighboring Deià and the nearby estate Son Marroig, which was the home of Archduke Luis Salvador of Austria, considered a great benefactor of Mallorca. Before his death in 1915, he had bought and restored many old mansions, and also had collected and saved antiquities and catalogued the plant life of the island.

Sóller also presents many musical events and, in addition, has a very well trained folkloric dance and music company, Aires Sollerics. (Earlier there was the Brot de Taronger [Branch of the Orange Tree].) One day in the 50's the members arrived at Villa Rua and were all thrilled to speak and sing and then hear their own voices on Escha's wire recorder, a recording machine which was in use before the tape recorder came on the market.)

Every summer Aires Sollerics host a festival, Mostra Internacional Folklòrica, in which six or seven other groups from all over the world participate. One year I was attached to and responsible for the Swedish dancers. About twenty-five years ago when Ceausescu was still in power, a Rumanian pair, Agnes and Dumitru, decided to defect and remain on the island. The night before their group was to leave he stole into the political officer's room to get their passports. They then stealthily left the center where all the other participants were and ran down the trolley tracks to the house which had been offered to them as a refuge by an American couple, the Bishops, terrified that they would be followed by police and dogs. In the following days they saw the authorities in Sóller and Palma and were finally accepted as political refugees. After the death of Ceausescu some years later they were able to visit their families in Rumania. None of their letters home had been delivered during his regime, and their families had suffered various indignities.

I must include here an episode that occurred when I visited the couple shortly after they had settled in. Dumitru spoke English fairly well and some Spanish; his companion had studied English in school but was shy about using it, so he interpreted for us both. At one point, however, after Agnes had turned to him with a question in Rumanian for me, I answered immediately without his intervention. We all looked at one another amazed that I had understood her but, after all, it is a Romance language, so some words are similar to Spanish, French and Latin, all of which I had studied.

Sóller also can boast of its Casal de Cultura and its museum and the prestigious Balearic Museum of Natural Sciences and Botanical Gardens, founded in 1992 .

One afternoon a month or so after I arrived in 1959, I set off for a walk up the "American" or "new" road, as it was known. A military base, one of a chain run jointly by Spaniards and Americans, had been installed on the top of the Puig Major, the highest peak on Mallorca, and a road up from Sóller to the base and then across the island was under construction. The base was supposed to be a secret; but as hikers and picnickers were no longer permitted at the top, word got around though no one seemed to know what the purpose of the base was. One heard all sorts of rumors: radar station, missile base, what? But whatever it was the local people were not enthusiastic about it. A few Mallorquíns got jobs there, but the economy of the community did not benefit because the Americans did not buy any of their food or other supplies in Sóller as everything was flown in. At one time there were some two to three hundred

Sell your books at World of Books!
Go to sell.worldofbooks.com and get an instant price quote. We even pay the shipping - see what your old books are worth today!

Inspected By: francisco_bibriescas

00086132599

0008613 **2599** c-2

S-4

Sell your books at
World of Books!
Go to sell.worldofbooks.com
and get an instant price
quote. We even pay the
shipping - see what your old
books are worth today!

0086132599

2599 C-2

0086132

S-4

American airmen based on the Puig, as well as Spaniards, but the commanding colonel was Spanish.

The workmen on the new road were Spaniards -- including, in fact, the husband and older son of my Cruz (unknown to me then) who had come over from Murcia to find work – but the engineering and financial support were American. Some of the workers seemed lackadaisical – well, it was a very hot afternoon -- and I thought it odd that at 3:30 a few were still having a siesta. Where was the foreman? When I called out a *"buenas tardes,"* they looked up surprised to see a foreign woman on the rough terrain.

As I worked my way along under the sun, I developed a great thirst; so when one of the workmen offered me his *porrón*, a leather water bottle, I was happy to accept. But to drink from it you are supposed to raise it above your head and tip it so the water flows from the narrow spout and into your open mouth without the spout's touching it. I'd never done this before and assumed that if I tried, I'd end up drenched. As I hesitated, the man offered me the other side of the bottle which had a mouth. I did not know who had drunk from it before, but my American ideas of what was sanitary or not sanitary did not stop me from quenching my thirst. He and I exchanged smiles, and I continued up the road to the turnoff down to Fornalutx, then back to Sóller, a distance altogether of some ten or twelve kilometers.

Nowadays you almost never see a *porrón*. One of our favorite restaurants used to offer one with muscatel to all the diners at the end of their meals (though it was chiefly the men who drank), but, alas, that custom has died out.

We few American residents in the valley were often invited to the base on American holidays, such as the Fourth of July, and at one event I was asked to give a short welcome speech and interpret for the Spanish speakers. In the canteen I was appalled at the wastefulness of the Americans who loaded their plates with steaks, chops, roasted meat or whatever and frequently left half of the food uneaten. There were many people in Sóller who could not afford to buy much meat. The Puig Major was considered a hardship base by the Americans inasmuch as it had no PX though the men could order items from a base on the mainland. The beautiful scenery and the opportunity to become acquainted with another culture apparently counted for nothing. Most of the men were not interested; except for a very few they did not attempt to learn Spanish, but I did have a group who came to me for lessons.

I was disappointed in the low level of general education these men had (I am not referring to their technical knowledge about which I knew nothing). Gradually they fell away one by one. Perhaps I was the wrong teacher for them; they certainly did not want to do any homework and did not appear to learn very much.

Joe, another young airman who came for Spanish lessons, was quite different. He was bright and we got on very well. He was an inductee not very pleased with his job, and he did not fit in with most of the other men. In addition, the commanding American officer was a young lieutenant who was new to his position and took it very seriously. He issued an order that any airman leaving the base and wearing sandals had to wear socks also. (No American was allowed to go off base in uniform. I think this had to do with trying to keep the local people from knowing there was a base on the Puig and Americans assigned to it! But of course it was common knowledge.) My young friend thought that his superior's ruling was stupid, so he deliberately disobeyed it. Joe told me that the lieutenant could not possibly have him court-martialed on the basis of his having disobeyed an order to wear socks (even he knew that would make him look ridiculous), but he did have the airman kicked out of the Air Force with a discharge without honor. Joe was delighted, he said, as he had wanted to leave the service anyway. The American military left the base in September, 1988, but a few civilian technicians stayed on until the end of 1993.

As Escha was very occupied with her writing and music -- the neighborhood children who had undoubtedly never heard the violin played live, or otherwise, used to stand outside Villa Rua in rapt attention when Escha was practicing. One man nearby would bring his violin to her to tune as he could not do it himself -- I generally did the morning shopping and errands which gave me the opportunity to practice my Spanish. I walked up the tracks to the town and back, being careful to avoid the trolley schedule. One day after selecting some fruit and vegetables at a stand in the market, I realized that I'd left our household purse at home and told the vender I could not take the things as I had no money with me. She laughed, told me to pay the next time and insisted that I borrow five hundred pesetas so I could do the rest of my shopping elsewhere.

We sometimes found it difficult to cope with the fact that an appointment for a certain hour did not mean that a person was committed to show up at that time. When you called the plumber or electrician to come, he would invariably ask if you would be home that afternoon or evening and imply that he would come then but that did not ensure that he would actually do so. It was not considered polite for him to give a negative answer. We should have preferred that he say frankly, "I can't come today or tomorrow, but I will come next Tuesday/ Friday morning (or whenever)" and actually arrive at that time. In those days no one charged for travel time, and generally everyone worked hard, in spite of the idea of *mañana*. Although unkept appointments could be a nuisance, the friendliness and helpfulness of the people helped to make up for them. And there was another plus to this relaxed attitude toward time: It was a pleasure in a restaurant not to have the bill presented and be rushed out the minute we finished eating. We could sit and chat as long as we wanted to, and we still can.

One day shortly after I came to live here, I went to Palma on various errands. One was to have the handle of a rather special leather bag repaired, and this was something I wanted to accomplish on my own even with my limited Spanish. I inquired at a shop that sold bags, and the proprietor told me she could not do it but there was someone who could. Thinking that as a stranger I might get lost on the way, she sent her young assistant to take me to the other store. I could not believe it, but that was only the first of many such kindnesses shown to me and to other foreigners by local people.

On that same day I had an extraordinary experience. When I had lived in midtown New York, many mornings when I left my apartment to walk to my office, I saw two middleaged women, obviously twins, dressed identically, even to shoes and handbags, who lived on the street next to mine. In Palma that day suddenly I saw the same two women, still identically clothed, and I stopped them to say, "How unusual to see you here. Do you still live on East 53rd Street?" They stared at me in astonishment, then one said, "Yes, we do, but how do you know us, how do you recognize us?" I explained as tactfully as possible without saying that it was their manner of dress that had drawn my attention.

A close friend of Escha's from the United States came to visit her for a few days. He overslept the morning of his departure, waking only as he heard the early morning trolley pass the nearby stop on the way up to the station, the trolley he should have caught in order to make the 6:45 a.m. train to Palma and then his plane. As he threw on his clothes, Escha raced up the lane, across the tracks and to the main road. She hailed a motorcyclist and begged him to take her guest to the station. Freddy was very tall, but he perched on the back with one suitcase under each arm, the cyclist roared off and got Freddy to the station just in time. The young man would not accept a peseta. What a wonderful place to live!

Many Americans who had heard of Mallorca but knew relatively little about it thought that it was a year-round summer resort. (Not so surprising when you consider that even the editor of the island's English newspaper recently ran an editorial indicating that the climate was temperate all year around.) I, too, had had the mistaken impression that the island enjoyed a sub-tropical climate (my geographical sense is poor until I visit a place, and I had not realized that Mallorca is on almost the same lattitude as New York and had many of the same flowers that I was familiar with, as well as others that grow in a warmer climate.) One winter's day when it was raining and the thermometer registered some five degrees Centigrade (41 degrees Fahrenheit), I received a letter from a Massachusetts friend who pictured me sitting on the beach under an umbrella to protect me from the sun. I answered that letter more quickly than I had ever replied to anyone before.

In April, 1974, the low areas between La Huerta and the port were inundated; houses were damaged, crops lost and small animals killed. In winter there is snow on the mountain tops very often, and every four or five years we actually have snow on the streets of Fornalutx – this does not occur very often in Sóller which is at sea level. Many children have never seen mounds of snow, so every time there is a heavy snowfall on the mountains, families from all over come to see it. When this occurred in March, 2004, with the thermometer registering zero degrees Centigrade and the entire valley covered in a thick white blanket, some 8,000 vehicles passed through the tunnel from Palma and other towns on the way up to the mountains to see the magnificent sight.

My first December here, in 1959, it actually rained on twenty-nine of its thirty-one days. The nearby *torrente* -- there are no rivers on Mallorca -- was full and roaring, and one day when I was carrying two full shopping baskets I crossed the trolley bridge near Villa Rua with trepidation. It was shorter to go that way instead of on the road, but I never did it again when the water was lapping at the bottom of the ties.

Summers were generally good but some of the British found the heat of July and August too much for them, and they spent that period in England. In 1957 during my five weeks' stay in May and June, however, it was unseasonably cold. No Mallorquin woman wore slacks then, but Escha always did though she covered them with a long coat when she went up to the town. I had brought only warm-weather clothes, so I had to borrow slacks from Escha who was some eight inches taller than I, rolling them down at the waist and up at the ankles. Comfort was more important to me than style then, and it probably still is. On the 10th of June of that year we had to light a fire in one of the fireplaces, the only method of heat that the house was blessed with, except for a "camilla," a round table with a brazier holding burning charcoal underneath. The warm cloth over the table was long enough to cover your knees and feet, so that your front was warm, leaving your back in the chill.

But the weather could change very quickly. During the first summer I lived in Spain we had a brief but disastrous hailstorm on the fifteenth of July which destroyed a good part of the fruit crop. On the other hand, June, 2003, was the hottest on record and July, 2006, the hottest in forty years, followed by the second coolest August in fifteen years. There is no doubt that in the past half century the climate has changed here. The *torrente* in the early days was usually full from November or December till April or so, but now the level of water is seldom very high, except for a couple of winter months.

In November, 1964, the Majorca Daily Bulletin printed a letter from the then editor in reply to a request for a weather forecast: "If we haven't carried forecasts before it is because in summer we get nothing but long hours of sunshine and in winter the residents know what the day is going to be like."!!

While most Christmases were days to be celebrated indoors, occasionally we were lucky enough to be able to sit outside for lunch. On New Years Eve in 1960, however, it was very cold. We were invited to a party at the Wrights' house in the area known as Binibassi and we knew they made little effort to heat it. In fact, I am not sure if they had any form of heat in the place. Before dressing that evening, we had quite a discussion and finally said, "To hell with the proprieties." We both wore warm slacks instead of dresses, the only women who did, and probably were the only comfortable ones there.

Perhaps the best Christmas Day I have ever experienced occurred in 1961. We had made friends with Rosa and Carla who had arrived from western Australia where they had lived for five years. Rosa, English, had studied design and during the Second World War had worked at the Admiralty on weather maps for the invasion. Carla was Dutch, a nurse, and she had gone to England to work as an "*au pair*" so she could improve her knowledge of the language. They had met in London, become friends and then had decided to emigrate to Australia. Carla had no difficulty in finding work there, but it was a different picture for Rosa who was fifteen years older. At that time Australia had a very *macho* society with the emphasis on youth. At any rate, while there they had heard a radio broadcast from someone who described the little village in Mallorca where he had bought some ruined houses and rebuilt and renovated them, so they met this chap and on the basis of what he told them decided to pack up their belongings and come over here with their big dog by ship. When Escha and I met them they were living in a room in Sóller and in the process of buying a *finca* [property] with a ruin on it. Rosa and Carla spent that summer sleeping in two tents while the house was being reconstructed. When it rained once in a while they, the dog and the two kittens they had rescued from the *torrente* took refuge in the tents. Rosa could handle many tools as well as most men, so she worked along with them, much to their amazement and, perhaps, consternation. It was not the sort of behavior one expected of *señoras*. Carla carried, ran errands, cleaned and made herself generally useful, and a few of the rooms were ready for them to move into when the cold weather arrived.

The two women had their hearts set on celebrating Christmas in their new home and invited a small group of new friends to share it with them. As none of us had much money at that time, all eight of us contributed to the feast, one bringing vegetables, someone else olives, nuts and other extras, the wine being the responsibility of a third person and so on. The hostesses had expected to get a turkey and have it roasted at the baker's as was the local custom, but for some reason a turkey was not available. They, therefore, bought two chickens, and Rosa built a small oven of bricks and I-don't-know-what-else, and on Christmas morning they put the pot with the two birds on an electric hot plate in the oven. By 8 p.m. the chickens were roasted. That meal was certainly one of the best of my life.

Carla had grown up through hard times in Holland during the war though she was more fortunate than some of her countrymen. Her father was a civil servant and, as such, was allowed with his family to continue living in his home, albeit in the attic while German officers took over the rest of the house. Carla was always hungry as she shot up in height in her teens, and food was scarce although occasionally one of the officers would present them with a welcome addition to their table. For the rest of her life she never wasted a crumb or anything else. If she saw horse manure in the road, she stopped at once, shoveled it into a special container carried for this purpose and took it home to be used to help fertilize their plants and trees.

It was a sad day for me in late 1990 when Rosa and Carla told me of their decision to sell up and move back to England.

Rosa had had a couple of strokes and Carla had a physical problem which was dragging on. They had never wanted a phone but now they felt one was necessary in case of emergency as their house was isolated. Unfortunately there was still a waiting list with Telefónica. Also Rosa felt at a disadvantage in treating with medical staff as her Spanish was rudimentary. They hated the idea of giving up their home in Sóller but reluctantly faced reality, and so they left the valley in January, 1991.

Although most families had a *belén* [crèche], some of which were very old and ornate and had beautiful carved fiigures, Christmas Day was not a real holiday in the early days, and the shops were all open. Christmas cards were not available until some years later, and then at first only very simple ones about a week or ten days beforehand. It was the following day, the 26th of December, which was celebrated though most people went to midnight mass on Christmas Eve when the "*Sibil.la*" was sung by a boy soprano. After the mass people generally went to a café to have hot chocolate and "*ensaimadas*", a light round-ringed pastry covered with powdered sugar. For the children, of course, the most important time was, and still is, the evening of the fifth of January when Los Reyes [the Three Kings] brought the presents. Each village and town had its own way of arranging this ceremony. In Fornalutx the Kings arrived on horseback, went up the steps and entered the church. Later the presents, which the families had bought and previously delivered to a set place, were taken by the Kings to the children's houses. As the years passed, Christmas Day became more important, and very little work is done from Christmas Eve to the seventh of January.

A word or two about the singing of the *Sibil.la*, a ceremony unique to Mallorca and one place in Sardinia. The name means the prophesies of the Day of Judgment and the Second Coming of Christ. The boy singer represented the Sybil, or prophetess, and was dressed in Oriental robes and carried a sword. Now girl or even a woman may be the singer of this quarter-tone Arabic music.

MAKING A LIVING

During my first summer in 1959 I went to the beach regularly. In September or October a young man whom I had met while swimming came to the door and said, "You teach English, don't you?" I thought for a few seconds, gulped, then answered in the affirmative; after all, I had been looking for a way to earn a living. He asked me what I charged and I told him three hundred pesetas a month (less then two euros) which was what I had paid for my Spanish lessons. When he came the following week, he brought a friend with him and said he assumed that each would pay one hundred and fifty pesetas. Out of ignorance I agreed, not realizing that for two each should pay somewhat more than half the single rate. This young man was very apt and knew a fair amount of English. One day he asked me to explain the difference among the verbs "to grasp, to clutch, to grab, to clasp, to seize, to grip" and a few more. I earned my money that day.

Although I had trained people in office procedures, taught a couple of children to swim and tutored in Latin many years ago, teaching a living language was new to me. At first I was not a very good teacher, but my students were not aware of this as they had not been spoiled in this area. Part of my problem was that they all thought in Mallorquín and I used Castilian in my explanations – I would have caused great frustration and undoubtedly wasted all of my students' time if I had confined myself to English only. In addition, my expectations were too high. I tried various books (today's methods were not available) until I worked out a good system, and over the years I devised many useful materials. I knew that I should teach not American English but English English as that was what most of the tourists spoke; but this was not a real problem for me inasmuch as the books I used were published in England. In addition, my father was a Londoner and I had grown up hearing his English. (Nonetheless, I decided to employ American usage in this book.)

There was one exception among my students, a youngster of fourteen or so who had begun to work with the Americans on the base on the Puig Major, so with him I used Americanisms. After he became a skilled electrician, he did the installation in my house, continuing for many years to come for lessons, which were chiefly conversational exchanges. We discussed many subjects, such as politics, sexual customs, religion and so on, that he said he had never been able to talk about with anyone else. I learned a great deal about Mallorquín life from him, too. The evening of his one thousandth lesson, I gave him a surprise party, the other guests being friends of mine for whom he had done electrical jobs. While he never did learn to write English very well – not surprising inasmuch as at school he'd never had to compose a paragraph or more in Spanish – he could speak and understand English quite well. This is something he never let his boss on the base know, so he was often present when meetings took place and matters discussed in English that he had no right to know about.

When this young man married, he did me the honor of

saying that he would like me to be the godmother of his first child. When the time came, however, a member of the family took on that responsibility which I felt was appropriate.

Parenthetical note: One day last year I met the wife of this ex-student of mine. She told me that their daughter was then twenty-five and their son, twenty-seven. He had obtained a doctorate. This is a wonderful example of the great difference in educational opportunities available from one generation to another in this country.

A couple of months after I began to teach, I realized that I ought to have a blackboard. At first, though it seems incredible to me now, I was very shy about standing up and writing on it. Fortunately, my students did not catch on to this, and soon I felt completely comfortable and could write and draw with ease (though I would never win a prize for my artistic endeavors).

Although my students spoke Mallorquín fluently and thought in that language, most could not write it as it was not taught during Franco's regime. They also spoke Castilian, the official language of Spain then; but as many left school at an early age, they did not write it well (and many of their parents could barely do so). I, on the other hand, was certainly not fluent in Spanish when I began teaching and had little knowledge of Mallorquín. I wanted to teach English in all its aspects: to read and to write as well as to speak it whereas a good many of those who came for lessons were interested only in being able to *"defenderse"* in conversation, that is, to learn enough to understand and to communicate with the tourists even if only on an elementary level.

Because of censorship of the media, their knowledge of

the world outside of Spain was limited, so sometimes it was difficult to explain an idea; and there were some who found English too difficult or who seemed to expect me to do the work while they sat there expending no effort. After a full day of preparing lessons and teaching such youngsters, I often felt that I could not cope with such an existence. Then, however, I would ask myself, "Do you really want to go back to the United States and the pressures under which you lived there?" That self-examination was usually sufficient to stop my complaints.

One of my students, Pau, was a twenty-eight-year-old man who bicycled down from Fornalutx to Sóller one evening a week after work, but he had to have permission from his father to use the bicycle! He was close to being illiterate, but he had ordered a little book from a Barcelona firm which purported to teach English. Normally I would not have used this method as I had my own system and books, but Pau wanted only to learn enough to chat up the English summer female visitors, and I was sure my material would be too difficult for him. I took him on and found teaching him a novel experience. He was quite bright but almost everything written was new to him. For instance, when I wrote on the blackboard the first time, he said, "Oh, that is very interesting."

"What is interesting?"

"It looks just like the letters in the book." It took me a few seconds to realize he was fascinated by my printed words – I printed each letter because I thought that my handwriting might not be legible enough. I taught Pau what he wanted to know: He could make a bit of conversation with a young woman, invite her to have a drink or to dance, and even to escort her to her room. After that he was on his own!

Pau lived in a house without indoor plumbing and obviously had not been taught some of the manners we take for granted. The first time he came for a lesson he sat with his beret on and flipped his cigarette ashes on the floor. I indicated the ashtray to him and said, "You know, Pau, customs differ in each country. In a private home in England you do not flip your ashes on the floor, and a gentleman takes his hat (or beret) off in the house."

"Oh, thank you, *señora,*" and he hastily removed his beret.

Another time he asked if he could use the lavatory. He left the door to the hall open as well as the bathroom door. When he came back, I said again, "Pau, customs are different in different countries. In England you always close the bathroom door." And again, "Thank you, *señora.*" He was quite goodlooking, but I have a feeling that Pau, eager though he was to learn, made no conquests among the visitors.

Another 18-year-old who came from Madrid literally did not know where in a notebook he should write: on page one, the back page, in the middle? He came with two or three others but could not keep up with them so soon gave up classes. In fact, a number of students did not continue beyond a few months as they had not understood that to learn English or any language they would have to do more than sit passively. Frequently when I asked a student to make a sentence with a certain word, she would think a minute and then quote a sentence from the book. I would reply that it was a good sentence but I wanted her to think of one of her own. This almost always stumped the student as the method of teaching here required students to memorize and repeat material from their books. When I put objects on the table and moved them about to demonstrate the use of certain words, they were surprised and silent. I had summer students who had studied English for three or four years but literally could not pronounce a single word even if they could do written translations fairly well.

Two of the best students I ever had were a brother of nine and a sister of eleven. They came in the summer because their days were fully occupied during the school year. However, in the tourist season they had to help out in the family restaurant; and young as they were, they worked in the evenings, the eleven-year-old until an hour later than her brother. Their only time available for classes was at 9 a.m. and the poor kids were always sleepy. Nevertheless, they were a joy to teach and picked up everything very quickly. One usage in English which was difficult for most of my students was the possessive case and use of the apostrophe in a phrase, such as, "my brother's book". This does not exist in Spanish or in many other languages. These youngsters understood immediately. Perhaps a minor matter but it made an impression on me.

Almost never did a student who could not come for a lesson advise me in advance. In some cases a telephone was not available, but in others I believe that it simply did not occur to them to do so. If I did get a call, I might hear, "This is Margarita (or Pep)," but no last name, and I would have to guess which one of the two or three of my students of that name it was. I had the same problem when a woman would stop me in Sóller and ask, "How is my Catalina doing?" (They almost always used the verb *comportar* which means to behave.) In many cases I was not sure who she or her Catalina was, but I always answered, "Very well." If she looked a bit dubious, I would add,

"But, you know, English is difficult to learn. It takes time." This usually relaxed the questioner.

After a couple of years of teaching during which the number of my students increased considerably, I recognized that I should formalize my position, so in January, 1962, I registered in Palma as a *profesora de idiomas* – that did not mean that I was a professor but simply a teacher of languages. I also received my work permit.. During the next year or so, various problems developed due to records being lost and mix-ups between offices. Two or three times a *guardia civil* delivered a notice advising me to present myself in Palma with receipts and other papers. A lawyer friend of mine did his best to straighten things out, and he was eventually successful.

In addition, it was obligatory that I be interviewed, sign up for and pay into the national pension fund as a self-employed person. This also had to be done in Palma, and the local *gestor* went with me. (There is no American or English equivalent of a *gestor*; perhaps the nearest is the French *homme d'affaires*. He has had legal training but does not work as a lawyer; he may prepare papers for you to obtain an identity card or help you to make your tax declaration or arrange documents for the sale of your car, et cetera.) One of the questions asked of me during the interview was "How long have you been teaching?" I thought the answer might affect the amount or the length of time I would have to pay into the fund, and I knew that no one told the exact truth here on official matters. The trouble was that I did not know whether it was better to have been teaching a short or a longer time, so I mumbled something about a few months. That turned out to be fine because if I had said, "Two or three years," I should have had to pay retroactively for the entire period.

The manner of levying taxes on my teaching income was curious, to say the least. A Sóller policeman usually delivered an unsealed document addressed to me, which indicated how much tax I had to pay for the preceding, or sometimes second preceding, year. This paper listed all the registered teachers of languages in the Balearic Islands in order of their supposed income. There were a number of columns; in the first a name, in the second that person's income, then sums deducted, percentages of I-did-not-know-what, and in the final column the tax due, though for some names this was a zero. I never found out the basis for the income figures; I had certainly never supplied any such information and the amount did not bear any relationship to what I had actually earned. Each name remained in its place on the list year after year, one of a number in a group with the same income.

After I had paid this tax for some years, I asked my former teacher of Spanish, who had a zero in the final column, how she had obtained it. She sent me to see a *gestor* in Palma. He asked me whether I had signed such and such a form. I hadn't. He slapped down a copy and said, "Sign it." I did. After that in the annual list of taxes due, my name was followed by a zero.

A few times I received an official notice of a meeting in Palma of all the language teachers. Although I had to cancel lessons (which later I had to make up as my students paid me monthly in advance), I went two or three times but did not honestly understand what the government representative was talking about. As only four or five other teachers bothered to show up and nothing seemed to be accomplished, I did not go again. The notices stopped arriving a couple of years later.

To avoid having to go to Palma just to pick up the application forms needed to renew my work permit, one year I wrote to the appropriate office, enclosing a stamped, self-addressed envelope and more than enough stamps to cover the cost of the forms (yes, they charged for them and you pay for income tax declaration forms, too) and asked them to mail the forms to me. They did not reply so I had to go fetch them. When I turned them in, I asked the clerk why they had not responded to my letter. He was a short man, not much taller then I, but he figuratively drew himself up to a great height and responded, "*Señora*, we are much too busy to answer all the letters that arrive at this office." My own feeling was that it was a rare day when more than one letter was received there, and I was annoyed so I said something extremely foolish: "In my country government employees answer their mail."

The man gave me a sharp look, then examined the papers I had submitted. I knew I was in trouble when he said, "You have declared a very small income. You can't live on that. What other income have you?" My reported income had not been questioned before even though, following local custom, I had never given the correct figure. I thought a minute, then told him I had help from my family and also ran a little lending library. "Ah, and have you a work permit for that?" Well, of course, I did not. He gave me a batch of forms and told me to fill them out and bring them back promptly, which I did not do. The following year when I returned to the office, I was sure I'd have a difficult time. To my pleased amazement, this man who had always been gruff and brusque was in a fine mood and undoubtedly did not remember the occurrence of the previous year.

When I was in my 60's, I decided to give up teaching. By then, I was living in Fornalutx and I had few students as it was not convenient for many young people to come up from Sóller for lessons. The schedule of those few often interfered with the house management responsibilities which had begun to occupy so much of my time. I therefore went to the Hacienda [tax office] in Palma to have my name taken off the books as a teacher. An official typed up a document which I signed. When I asked for my copy, he said he had not made one for me, and there was no copier in the office. Not to worry, he said, if any question came up in the future, all I need do was to come to see him or his associate to whom he introduced me. A few years later I received tax bills plus interest for the two years following my visit to the Hacienda. I went to Palma to protest, only to be told that both men had been transferred to mainland Spain. There was no record of the declaration I had signed. My lawyer friend then accompanied me to see the director of the Palma office, whom he knew. This gentleman was very polite but said the document could not be found even though I had given him the date and the names of the two officials. Gently he said, "I am very sorry. *Usted tiene toda la razón, pero tendrá que pagar.*" ["You are completely right, but you will have to pay."] And pay I did.

Many young people could not understand why I and other foreigners would prefer to live in a small town like Sóller instead of in London or New York which represented to them opportunity and luxury and freedom. What they knew of the outside world they had learned from movies. When I spoke of the beauty of the valley, the tranquillity, the fact there was no crime, the friendliness of a small place, they were not convinced. Developing tourism – actual contact with people from abroad -- was helping them to open their eyes to life outside Spain. They knew their lives were limited in many ways, and they yearned to leave the limitations placed upon them by government regulations, family responsibilities or lack of financial resources. Certainly most of them did not want to continue to try to earn an uncertain living from the land (some years the farmers left lemons on the ground to rot as it was not worth their while to harvest them), and some had dreams of going abroad. Under Franco, however, before they could apply for a passport, young men had to do their military service and women to complete what was known as *servicio social*. Classes in cooking, sewing and embroidery and religion were included in the latter. In addition, married women needed permission from their husbands and single women up to the age of twenty-one, from their fathers. Fortunately, all of that is now a thing of the past.

Some young women here told me they would prefer to marry Englishmen rather than Mallorquíns. Why, I asked. "Because we have seen how the English go shopping with their wives and help them to carry their purchases home, and they apparently do not consider themselves superior to women. They do not throw their weight around, as our men do." Still, I know a number of English women who have married or are paired happily with Spaniards, but these men may not be typical.

There is no doubt that males were favored over females in many areas. Conditions are much better today, of course. Sóller has for some years had a number of women on its municipal police force, and in the summer of 2006 the first woman was appointed to the Sóller headquarters of the Guardia Civil. There are many women doctors, dentists, engineers, lawyers and government officials in Spain. When the Socialists took power in the last national elections, the new prime minister, José Luis Rodriguez Zapatero, named eight women to his sixteen-member cabinet, and the Deputy Prime Minister is also a woman. He chooses to be known by the surname of his mother and not of his father. Nonetheless, machismo still exists; pictures of local councils, committees or commissions which appear in newspapers usually feature no women or only a token one or two. An exception might be in the field of social services. Obviously, it is not only in Spain where *machismo* persists; I am a tennis nut and see as much tennis on TV as I can. There are a few women chair umpires who almost always take charge of women's matches but only rarely of men's whereas men umpires work at matches of both sexes.

In my early years here I often saw the only male customer in a butcher's or grocer's be attended to ahead of his turn. But that also happened to me as a foreigner at first until I politely refused the courtesy. Among my students I had a highly intelligent brother and sister who both wanted a university education. Their mother whose husband had deserted her and the children had a hard time making ends meet. While attendance at a university was free the books, which were very expensive, and lodging were not; so only one child in this family could receive a higher education, and it automatically fell to the boy . That young woman was very disappointed and I shared her feelings.

Compulsory military service, which was abolished in 2001, was not something young men looked forward to. The uniforms were bulky and often did not fit, the food was sometimes very skimpy, and in the early 60's the monthly salary was only fifteen pesetas a month! Even the cheapest cigarettes, Ideales, cost two and a half pesetas for a pack of eighteen; they were made of coarse tobacco wrapped in a yellowish paper. (After trying them I switched to Renos which were mentholated, at three pesetas for twenty.) The youngsters I knew hoped they would be assigned to the Puig Major base and not sent to the mainland, so they could get home occasionally and have a decent meal. When they returned to duty, they often carried a package of home-cooked food with them.

One of my students, a big fellow, said he'd never have survived on the official rations. He was lucky enough to receive a special assignment situated off base in the mountains; for some reason, probably a mistake on someone's part, he and his group of five or six received rations for double that number, so they were luckier than others.

Many of the local people were resentful of the Spanish Air Force officers serving on the Puig, and one day I saw the reason for that feeling. I was in a shop when a well dressed young woman entered, looked at some lipsticks and then, as the wife of an officer, asked for a discount. After she left, the shopkeeper expressed her indignation, saying they get free housing, their husbands' salaries are good, they enjoy privileges we do not – and they always want a discount on what they buy.

Those of my students who worked as receptionists at hotels saw the passports of their guests. One or two remarked to me how amazing it was that a carpenter or factory worker or store employee could afford a vacation abroad. They hoped that a knowledge of English would help them as they saw that the language was becoming more and more important as tourism developed. The local banks, shops and hotels wanted their employees to be able to understand and converse with the visitors. Restaurants began to produce menus in English as well as Spanish and French (Mallorquín could not be used during Franco's regime). But sometimes the knowledge of the language of the person making up the menu was limited or reference was made to a dictionary, and errors occurred. The most humorous one that I saw was a combination of typographical error and insufficient knowledge: "Rabbi on red hot wood." The "t" was later added to the first word so the poor man was no longer suffering.

With reference to annual vacations, I remember a conversation I had with a young woman. She had a job and like all workers in Spain received an extra month's salary on the first of July as well as on the first of December. When she got her July payment, I said innocently, "Now you can go away on vacation." "On, no, *señora*, I have to save the money for a winter coat." She was still living at home, however, and might not have been contributing very much to the family purse; many young adults did not so contribute.

You had to be discreet when discussing anyone as so many people were related. One day a student happened to look up and saw a big spiderweb hanging from the ceiling. I knew it was there and had been waiting to see how long it would take for my cleaning woman, whom I was not too fond of, to notice and remove it. I should have known better, but I made a slightly critical remark about her. The next morning she came roaring in and challenged me about what I had said. I had to wriggle out of that one, and it taught me a lesson.

All the Mallorquíns we dealt with were very honest. You could leave cash lying around and no one would touch it. And this was still in the days when you often went out without locking the door, or you left the key in the lock on the outside. But there was one exception, a young man who did certain jobs for us. We soon suspected that he was cheating us in small ways, and one time he went too far. He ordered a glass top for a table for us; and when it was delivered, he said it had cost two hundred and ninety-eight pesetas which he had paid on our behalf. This time Escha asked him for the receipt, but it was not forthcoming until she insisted. We saw then that the price had been changed from one hundred and ninety-eight pesetas. We let the matter go but he never worked for us again. Later this chap got into trouble over money stolen from a neighbor's house and ended up in jail.

That reminds me of a completely different episode. One time when I returned from a trip to England, I took a taxi from the airport to the garage in Sóller where I had left my car to be repaired during my absence. The driver took my suitcases out of the taxi, I paid him and he started back to Palma. A few seconds later I remembered the jacket I had taken off and thrown into the back seat –- I liked to ride next to the driver. I was unable to locate him because I did not have his name or number. As my small travel address and telephone book was in one of the jacket pockets, I was exceedingly sad to lose it, not to mention one of my favourite jackets. Two and a half months later, someone from the garage called me to say that a Palma taxi driver had dropped off a bag for me. When I picked it up, I found my jacket in it with the address book safe and sound. Alas, he did not leave his name but the garage people thought they knew which company employed him, so I called them to give him my thank you. He had obviously carried the bag around with him during all those months till he had a customer for Sóller.

BOOKS BOOKS BOOKS

While I was still casting about for a way to make a decent living, I was offered the opportunity to work as a guide on the excursion buses which toured the island. I went out twice with an experienced guide each time though I brought back one of the groups on my own. My "wages" were eight pesetas per tourist and, usually, a free lunch at the restaurant where we took the passengers. The guides told the tourists all kinds of interesting "facts", a good many of which were entertaining but untrue. I very soon realized that this type of employment was not for me as it would take up many hours for a small return.

Fortunately more students appeared and I gave up my studies of California real estate law as I saw the possibilities of a regular income, meager though it was. What I did not know was that lessons should have lasted only fifty or fifty-five minutes instead of the full hour I assigned, so that I would have a few minutes between students. There was one winter when I was teaching various hours six days a week, on two of which I had classes for ten full hours, plus other occupations.

The most important of my other occupations enabled me to enjoy to my heart's content what I liked doing best: reading. An Englishwoman who had run a rental library in the port had died, and Escha suggested that I might wish to take it on. The problem was lack of funds as I could not afford to rent space. I checked out various places and was delighted when Tofol of the Bar Turismo said, *"Ese idea me encanta,"* ["I am delighted by the idea."] and offered me a place in his bar.

Tofol, by the way, was self-educated (he had had to go to work at the age of fourteen), wrote poetry in Mallorquín and had a fine appreciation of good writing and art. He had some interesting paintings hanging in the bar. When he died years later of cancer, nine priests officiated at his funeral, probably arranged by his brother who was one of them; and the church may never have been so packed with not an inch of space unoccupied as a great many of his fellow townspeople wanted to do him honor. Tofol was not very religious, however, so I suspect he was sitting up in the clouds somewhere marvelling at the ceremony. We all missed him enormously.

When the books of the port library came up for sale, I found that most of them were dated and, I thought, unsuitable for my project. I offered to buy about one hundred of them, but the local lawyer handing the estate said they had to be sold on an all-or-none basis, so I left them. I had some book shelves made, arranged my own books and any others I was able to get hold of, including some that I knew were not going to be of interest but helped to fill up the shelves, to a total of approximately three hundred, and invited everyone I knew to the opening on September 10, 1963. Tofol very kindly told me to buy my "champagne" elsewhere as it would be more reasonable than if he supplied it. I bought a case of *cava* which was quite drinkable though the price was only eighteen pesetas a bottle.

As it happened, one of my friends fancied himself as a connoisseur of wine, as well as of art and music, and only three days before the opening of my library he had stated categorically that the only *cava* worth drinking was one which I knew cost three times as much as mine. I was afraid that he would taste it and make a show of spitting it out. Instead, he drank a number of glasses of it with evident enjoyment.

Every morning after my last student left, I jumped on my Mobylette with two baskets loaded with books in time to open the library at 11 a.m. In the bar I had room for only one thousand books or so, and regularly I replaced titles which had circulated well or for which there was no call with books from my house. As I got to know my readers, I had a pile of books for each one which I thought would be of interest, so most of them did not have to search for what they wanted to take out. I was at the library daily until 12:30 p.m. or a bit later if necessary and two days a week from 5 to 6 p.m., but I soon gave up the afternoon hours as they proved to be a waste of time. Many years later when I moved to Fornalutx I again had a library hour three afternoons weekly but in my house where most of the then thousands of books were kept.

When I started the library I charged seven or ten pesetas a week, depending on the type of book. Later, of course, the rates went up, but I never could have made a living out of the library as the income was minuscule, and I had to spend an inordinate amount of time, not only at the library but at home in reading reviews, ordering books, repairing books, et cetera. But that did not give me cause to complain as I loved working with books. The first book charged out to anyone was Djuna Barnes' "Nightwood," and the first month's income was 288 pesetas, equal to less than two of today's euros.

Shortly after I opened for business, someone asked me for Len Deighton's "The IPCRESS File" —- I had never heard of the author or the book —- but when he described it, I realized that my little library was lacking a, to me, new kind of literature, that is, behind-the-Iron-Curtain spy stories. I felt the same deficiency when a tourist asked me for a love story, and I knew she meant something like "Mamie Zilch, Girl Nurse," which I did not have. I offered her a good book of fiction with a love interest, the author of which she obviously did not know but which she accepted but then floored me when she said, "My 14-year-old daughter also wants a love story." Again I reached for a book which I knew was not what she had in mind, but I wanted my books to circulate and hated to see anyone leave without some reading matter. They brought the books back a week later and surprisingly paid the charge without comment.

Very soon after this episode I went to a secondhand book store in Palma and bought six Barbara Cartlands or their equivalents, which took care of the "love story" gap, and I also found a copy of Deighton's book. Gradually I covered other lacks, such as, science fiction, so that I could satisfy the requests of almost everybody, adding at the same time to my knowledge of present-day English authors. Alan Sillitoe had lived in the valley and struggled to survive during the 50's. His "Saturday Night and Sunday Morning," published in 1958, was written here. I had my first plate of snails at Ruth and Alan's house though Escha had fobbed one off on me one evening when we were having a snack in the port; I thought it was a very peculiar-tasting anchovy and did not like it. The snails here have a very different flavour from the French ones, and it is really the sauce which is so important.

90

Occasionally I bought books about the island or by people we knew to rent or sell. The first and one of the most popular was "Viva Majorca," written by Robert Graves who had lived in Deià for many years, and illustrated by Paul Hogarth who had a house in Fornalutx. As this book was published in London and my library had not established credit anywhere in England, I just took a chance and sent in my order for three copies, hoping the publishers would be intrigued by hearing from what I called a "library and book shop" located in a bar in Sóller. Evidently they were as they sent me the books without asking for credit references. Eventually I must have ordered and sold at least two or three dozen copies. And I used this firm as a credit reference when I ordered books from the next publisher on my list. Also I sold many books on Mediterranean food and guides for hikers on the island, and sometimes I had postcards with local scenes for sale. I did not make much money on the library as I had to buy so many books year after year, and some were not too popular; but I met hundreds of people and made many friends – and, of course, I had a wide selection to satisfy my own needs.

One day after the library had been in existence for a few years and registered with the authorities as a "business," I received a notice regarding a tax I apparently should have been paying. I asked a well placed Mallorquín friend of mine about it and he said, "Forget it." About a year later when another notice arrived, he repeated his advice; but the third notice with its warning made me realize that I had to take it seriously. I presented myself at the appropriate office in Palma, received a stern lecture and was told I'd have to pay a fine. My heart sank as the library income did not allow for such extras. So I did something I almost hate to admit: I became the helpless and stupid female, declared my ignorance of the tax law and spoke in broken Spanish. And I stated honestly that the library was open only an hour and a half daily and exaggerated my absences from the island when it was closed. The official relented, handed me a number of tax forms to fill out for the preceding two or three years, told me how to explain the very low income I would report and said I would have to pay the resulting small tax but no fine. From then on I dutifully paid the amount due and had no further trouble. I wondered how my Mallorquín friend would have handled the situation, but perhaps as a well known lawyer of good family and a male, he would have paid nothing.

As the English-speaking community enlarged, more and more residents found their way to the Bar Turismo. A few came in every day, others dropped in three or four times a week for a coffee or conversation. But most of them were interested in books as well as the opportunity to socialize. Sometimes we had parties in the bar to celebrate a birthday or other event. For years I invited everyone I knew at noon on Christmas Eve to have a pre-holiday glass or so of champagne. On Saturdays the bar was often mobbed by both Mallorquíns and foreigners because Catalina, Tofol's wife, turned out very good *tapas*, including the best spinach *croquetas* in town which she would make to order for our parties. Sadly for us, Catalina reached the age when she decided enough was enough, and her *tapas* are no longer available.

Having the library led to further possibilities for increasing my income and to the making of many close friends. Occasionally an English couple would come into the Bar Turismo and rather hesitantly ask clearly and slowly, "Do you speak English?" I would reply briefly, "Yes," and they would then begin in simple language, until I had the decency to let them know that English was my mother tongue, to explain that they wanted to rent or buy a house or apartment, did I know of anything available? Many property owners had asked me to act as their agent as it was obviously easier for them to deal with an English speaker who knew the ropes here than with a local person who spoke little or no English. Once I became involved in such activities and developed a reputation, my workload increased considerably. Finally I held a great number of powers of attorney, two or three of which, I believe, are still in effect.

From the mid-90's on I gradually faced the fact that I would have to make the sad decision to close the library as readership had fallen away drastically now that English-language publications were available in many places, people had TVs and bars and discotheques offered entertainment. I therefore began to sell or otherwise dispose of some of my thousands of books. In 1998 after thirty-five years of operation the Sóller English Lending Library, which had been a meeting place for many of the English-speaking residents, ceased to exist.

NAMES, LANGUAGE, CUSTOMS

As long as Escha lived in Villa Rua, she had a visit on the first or second of every month from Don Miguel Casasnovas who arrived in late afternoon to collect the rent although never would he have stated that that was the purpose of his visit. With great formality she always offered him a glass of his "champagne" which was local brandy with sparkling water from a syphon bottle. They were both very serious about it, but then they laughed. He never drank more than one glass, but he made it last the full hour or so that he and Escha chatted. As he got up to leave, Escha handed him an envelope which he tucked into his shirt pocket without looking at it. Escha would never have been so crass as to hand him the cash openly, nor would he ever have opened the envelope to count the money in front of her.

Don Miguel was a gentleman of the old school who had been the mayor of Sóller many years before. He was not the owner of the property; it belonged to Doña María, his wife, but as was the custom and, in fact, the law, it was the husband who handled any business matters. Balearic law differed in certain aspects from that of the mainland. For instance, while the property a woman owned when she married was administered by her husband, he could not sell or transfer it to anyone else without her signature, and the earnings from such property were hers. This system dated back hundreds of years. While many husbands today may handle their wives' holdings, it is simply a matter of custom or agreement between the two, not a matter of law.

I was pleased to see that Paquita, in spite of the difference in their social position, spoke to Don Miguel as though they were equals and he did not seem to resent this. In opposition to this seeming feeling of equality between Mallorquíns of different backgrounds, I was disturbed by the fact that foreigners were addressed as *señor* or s*eñora* automatically whereas we were expected to call most of them by their given names, as they did among themselves. Again and again when I asked for someone's name, I would get, "María (or Tolo), señora," which would leave me with no idea of their last name. (This did not apply to people like Don Miguel, lawyers, doctors, the priests, the small percentage of educated people.) Even after I had been here for quite a while and had asked people to use my first name, many, particularly men, found it difficult to do so. A few still address me as Doña Elena (*don* and *doña* are courtesy titles). Also one Fornalutx resident continues to greet me in Mallorquín with, "*Bon día tenga*," which is very deferential. Young people are much more informal and use my first name easily, which I like..

That brings up the difference between the two words for "you," "*usted*" and "*tu*" (and also their plural forms) which can be puzzling to English speakers. Generally when you do not know the other person or are addressing someone senior to you in position or age, you use the word "*usted*" which takes the third person singular form of the verb. "*Tu*" indicates familiarity and is always used when speaking to members of the family, friends or to a child, but more and more it is adopted immediately people meet. It is interesting that Mallorquíns and perhaps all Spaniards are less formal than the French. I had a French friend whose mother was Spanish who always used the formal "*vous*" when speaking her tongue with me but automatically dropped into the informal "*tu*" when we conversed in Spanish.

On the subject of the use of first names, there was one notable exception in my life, Cruz, who looked after my house for almost thirty years until she retired at the age of eighty-one. She was born in Murcia, which was one of the poorest provinces of Spain, and went to work in a shoe factory when she was nine years old. She worked from 9 p.m. each night until 7 a.m. the following morning, with a half hour break for a snack. She is more or less illiterate, but she is thoughtful, intelligent and tolerant of other people's ideas. We often discussed politics or world affairs on which she is liberal. I was very lucky to have Cruz as my housekeeper for so long and was the envy of my friends.

A few years ago I asked her one morning, "Cruz, are you my friend?" To which she replied in astonishment, "But of course, I am, *señora*." Then I asked, "Am I your friend?" and she said, "I hope so, *señora*." I said I certainly was and pointed out that I called my friends by their first names and they called me Elena. "I want you also to call me Elena." "Oh, no, *señora*." "Yes, Cruz, I am Elena. Say it." "No, no, I couldn't."

I insisted for a few minutes, but it was no use. And her grown daughter sided with her mother. In spite of their reaction

I tried again but to no avail, so I had to drop the idea. And while many people here use the familiar "*tu*" with their employees, I always used the more formal "*usted*" with Cruz as she did with me as she was only nine years younger than I. With her daughter I used the familiar form.

I am not a natural linguist who picks up a language just by listening to others speaking it. Fortunately, my early studies of Latin and many years of French helped, though I had forgotten almost all of the former and a great deal of the latter. In Sóller a good proportion of the population spoke French through their connections with the fruit business in France, and many words in Mallorquín and that language are similar. It is the Arabic in Mallorquín which makes it somewhat difficult for us. Franco forbade the public use of any language but Spanish, but that did not prevent the local people from speaking their own tongue among themselves. However, while many could read it a bit, almost no one could write it as they had never been taught to do so. Now, of course, everyone here learns Catalan (or Mallorquín) as well as Spanish.

The four official languages of Spain are Castilian (Spanish), Basque, Galician and Catalan. Mallorquín is the local version of Catalan and very similar to it, but there are some differences in verb forms and vocabulary. In addition, there are variations in the pronunciation of vowels from town to town, and the natives of one village can spot someone from another by the way he pronounces, say, the "a" or "o." But these differences are fast disappearing. My house is called Ca Mestre Cinto [House of Master Cinto], this last name being the abbreviation of Jacinto -- he had been a master plumber -- and in this area the final "o" sounds like a "u." Ibicenco and Menorquín are also similar to Catalan with each having some of its own vocabulary.

When I ordered a name tile for my house some thirty-five years ago, the factory salesman said what I asked for, <u>Can</u> Mestre Cinto, was not correct, that it ought to be <u>Ca</u> Mestre Cinto; but he could not explain why or, if he did, I was unable to understand his explanation, so I had it made with Can, the name which had been given to me by the previous owner. However, after the tile was in place and two people had assured me that the first word was wrong, I capitulated and painted over the "n." Years later my teacher of Mallorquín clarified the matter: In Mallorca men have a courtesy title of *"en"* before their first names, thus, En Jordi or En Pep. Women use *"Na"* so you have Na Catalina. In certain cases these titles are shortened to N'. *"Ca"* and *"can"* mean "House of" but the latter must be followed by a man's first name. My house could have been named Can Cinto [House of En Cinto]; but the insertion of *Mestre* meant that the correct form was Ca Mestre Cinto. There are many other forms for the words "House of," and you may still see an apostrophe in words like Can and Cas, but the tendency now is to omit it.

As I wanted to learn a language I could use in any part of the country, I took lessons in Spanish on my two visits in 1955 and 1957; and a few months after my arrival in 1959 I buckled down to serious study as I like to communicate with people – I do have a reputation of being a talker! I have always loved grammar, so I spent considerable time on verbs and rules of usage. An English regular verb has only four forms, but a Spanish verb has almost sixty though a few are almost never used. One day shortly after I had learned the imperative form for reflexive and other types of verbs, I took the tram and met a Mallorquín acquaintance with her two children who were going to the beach. The ride to my stop lasted two or three minutes, all of which I needed to work out mentally how to say to the children, "Have a good time" ["*Divertíos*"], which looks simple and they took for granted but is rather complicated.

Of course, I picked up a little Mallorquín and would almost always greet people in it, but the majority of replies were in Spanish. They probably knew that I was not fluent in their tongue. Now that I have been here so long, many people speak to me in their language and assume that I understand them.

At first I did not know why so many people had the same first name: María, Pepe (for José), Cati (for Catalina). Pedro, Toni (for Antonio), Margarita. Had the parents no imagination? I soon learned the reasons: The first male child was named for his paternal grandfather; the first female child, for her paternal grandmother. The second boy, for his maternal grandfather; the second girl, for her maternal grandmother. All these were saints' names. This custom is no longer rigidly followed. In addition, children are now often given the Catalan version of a name, rather than the Spanish.

I was surprised the first time I came across a man called José María and a woman with the name María José as surely María was a woman and José a man. Of course, English also has dozens of names, such as Carey and Evelyn and Kim and many nicknames, which are used for both sexes, but the two Spanish names seemed different to me.

Foreigners are frequently confused by Spanish family names. If they see a combination of names, such as, José Arbona Mestre or Francisca Castañer Cortés, they think the way to address these people is as *Señor* Mestre or *Señora* Cortés ; but Spaniards have two surnames, the first being the father's and the second, the mother's. In the above cases he is Sr. Arbona and she is Sra. Castañer as the father's is used generally. If these two people were to marry, their children would have the two last names Arbona Castañer or, at least, they would have had until the 28th of February, 2000, when a law came into effect which permitted parents to register the mother's first family name followed by the father's, that is, the reverse of the previous custom.

Something else which confuses foreigners is the fact that a woman never loses her surnames when she marries, and she does not take her husband's family names except in formal society when the word "de" is added to hers, followed by her husband's. No one I know in my small village or the neighboring town follows this custom. When I had learned enough Spanish to try to read the local weekly newspaper, I was at first astonished at some of the social notes which might say something like this: "Don José Coll Pastor y Doña Margarita Ferrer Sastre have left to spend a week in Madrid." How, I wondered, could the paper publicize the fact that an unmarried couple had gone away together, and how could there be so many unmarried pairs in Sóller – remember, this was some forty or so years ago. Of course, they were all married couples which I did not realize then.

Many years ago there was a wedding announcement which created a small sensation. A man who had been a student of mine and who was a bit of a rebel had been living with a Scottish woman for some years when they decided to marry. They had a little girl. The local paper ran an announcement in which it was baldly stated that their daughter was the flower girl at the ceremony. I thought how upset they and their families must be until I was told that he himself had prepared the text.

Nowadays not many people would give such a statement a second thought.

With reference to the formation of last names, I saw a death notice in a Spanish paper some months ago. The deceased was the VIII *Marqués* de Campo-Franco, and he was named as *Ilmo.* [Most Illustrious] *Señor Don* Juan Miguel Roten Sureda de España y Fortuna (*Viudo* [Widower] de la *Ilma.* [Most Illustrious – feminine form] *Sra. Dña.* Ana de España Le-Senne). I admit that all of this almost defeated me, but there are even more complicated names when given in their entirety.

It was accepted by everyone years ago that the true value of a property was never declared as no one even considered the possibility of paying the correct amount of tax on any transaction. And in fact, most checks for payment to individuals were made out to *Portador* [Bearer] to protect anonymity, as are many today. In addition, when a check made out to a person's name was cashed, there was a charge of two or three pesetas which many people were unwilling to pay.

Banking and business procedures could involve a lot of red tape, but sometimes they were almost casual. At times this could be helpful but not always. One day in the 60's I had some cash to deposit, and the teller who had some paperwork to finish said he'd give me the receipt later – this was long before the age of the computer -- I knew him fairly well as he was a student of mine, but I felt a trifle uneasy until I had the paper.

When I was rebuilding the ruin I had bought in 1969, I sent

to the United States for money. I waited some weeks and still it did not arrive. My American bank assured me at least twice that the funds had been sent; the local bank blamed Madrid for the delay. Finally after two and a half months I insisted on some positive action from my bank. The man handling the matter shook his head negatively as he riffled through a batch of documents. "It isn't here, you know." Suddenly his face dropped as he pulled out a file of papers. Yes, there was the record of my funds having been received weeks before.

Escha had had a similar experience early in the 50's when she waited weeks for a transfer until she was desperate, only to be told finally that the papers had been found behind a radiator. On the other hand, if you were known to the local banks, they could be most helpful, even allowing certain transactions to go through without the required paperwork. On one occasion I withdrew funds from an account in Fornalutx over which I had power of attorney the day after the death of the account holder. Of course, such power expires with the death of the person, so legally I should not have still had access to the account, but I had to pay for her funeral and other expenses. The man at the bank asked if she were still alive and I told him honestly no, but I added, "But you have not been officially advised of this." He agreed to the withdrawal but he said he could not permit another one –- no problem for me as I had no intention of making another.

Almost every family with a bit of land kept one or two pigs that were living garbage cans as all food refuse was fed to them. If there were two, after the slaughter one was used to provide meat and sausages for months; but the other might be sold and the money received invested in gold as many people did not trust the banks. Usually in November the family invited as many relatives as possible, particularly the women, to come to what they called the sacrifice of a pig. The first time I was invited to a *matanzas* [pig slaughtering] I was somewhat hesitant, but fortunately I did not see the actual killing of the animal when its throat was cut and the blood collected for sausages. Big fig leaves were spread out on a long bench, and the parts of the animal were carefully washed and then laid out. To make *sobrasada*, the intestines were filled with meat chopped by machine and with red pepper which over a period of weeks and months would cure the uncooked meat. Nothing was wasted and in some households almost no other meat was available all winter unless they kept chickens and/or rabbits.

After one of the *matanzas*, as we were considered honored guests, we were given a bit of the fresh liver and some of the newly made *sobrasada* which I was urged to try, though I was somewhat dubious. And how right I was because shortly afterwards, I collapsed and hit my face on the stone terrace floor, which left me with a black eye. (My reaction was probably due to problems with my gall bladder which were diagnosed a few months later.) Unfortunately, while I still had the bruised eye, Escha's middle finger on her right hand was hit by the falling water tank in the bathroom, and for days we looked as though we had had a serious difference of opinion.

Most Mallorquíns, particularly the men and younger people, were not very religious. As Catholicism was the official religion of Spain until 1978, however (now, of course, there is complete religious freedom), they went through the motions and participated in at least four religious ceremonies: baptism, first communion, marriage and funeral. In my early years here a baby was usually baptized on the eighth or tenth day of its life with the mother often not present, and children had their first communions at the age of seven. Nowadays a child's baptism may be delayed for months or years as are first communions. Everyone who gets married must go through a civil service, and couples always had the legally required church wedding also. Times have changed: A report from the Spanish National Institute of Statistics covering the year 2003 states that in the Balearic Islands only fifth-eight per cent of marriages took place in a Catholic church. Also only half of the babies born on the islands were baptized in the church.

In spite of the lack of religious conviction among a good part of the populace, many local Catholic customs continued. For example, until the 70's or 80's or so a priest would come to bless an establishment, such as a bakery, the new post office, a clothing or shoe store at its opening ceremony. Each spring after Easter the parish priest visited all the houses in his community to bless them. Such activities, however, have fallen by the wayside in my area, at least. The word *paciencia* [patience] was used repeatedly and originally reflected, I think, the belief that hard though this life might be, there was a better one in Heaven to look forward to.

When anyone arrived at your house which was unlocked, he or she opened the door, sang out, *"Ave María Purísima"* and came in without waiting for an invitation. One day in 1959 a nun came to Villa Rua to give Escha an injection (the nunneries usually had one nun trained in this and other such procedures). Escha introduced us and as I knew that everyone shook hands on meeting, I put out my hand to shake hers. I do not know which one of us was more startled when I found myself grasping her crucifix which, I learned later, I had been expected to kiss. An awkward moment for both of us.

This was the same nun who was so shocked on seeing Judith come down the staircase dressed in a bikini as she was on her way to the back patio to sunbathe. The nun screamed, "Tell her to put on a skirt." I wonder what she would think if she could see the half-naked women on some of our beaches today.

Obviously some priests and nuns were stricter than others. Saturday night dances were forbidden by the priest of the church in neighboring Bunyola, so the young people used to come over the mountain to Sóller for their entertainment. On the other hand, Don Alfonso of Fornalutx, was very liberal, and many foreign residents, as well as Mallorquíns, were glad to take part in functions he sponsored.

I have been a participant in three Catholic weddings here (non-religious though I am), one in the Fornalutx church between two foreigners and two in Sóller. Twice I acted as translator, warning the priest beforehand to be sure that it was not I who ended up married! In the third wedding a friend and I substituted for the parents of the American groom who were unable to be present. What happened to this couple in the twenty-eight years they have been married is a wonderful story: The bride was only seventeen and she had not had much education, having left school at fourteen. In spite of having three children after the couple moved to the United States, she continued with her studies there, obtained a B.A. and then an M.A. and is now teaching at a university in the West. Her mother had been opposed to the marriage, possibly due to her daughter's youth, possibly because the groom was an American —- in fact, to show her disapproval she wore to the wedding an ordinary housedress and her husband, an opennecked shirt without tie -- but now she is surely proud of what her daughter has accomplished.

There was a fourth wedding ceremony between two Americans over which I "presided" in 2003; but as that had nothing to do with Mallorquín customs, I shall not describe that here.

A number of priests on Mallorca have during the past thirty years or so left the priesthood to get married, and I was a guest at the wedding of one of them. Don Alfonso shone as a priest and encouraged all people of whatever religion, or none, to participate in church activities, but he finally decided that he wished to marry and have a normal family life. He wrote to the Pope to ask for permission to leave the priesthood and marry but to remain a Catholic. While awaiting a reply, he gave up his religious duties. I met him in Sóller one day, and he told me that his letter to the Pope had been answered affirmatively. He and his bride, a local young woman, invited me to the wedding; they were married by a priest who was a friend of his in a private chapel near Pollensa. His oldfashioned mother, who always wore a black mantilla, was present though I understood that Alfonso had become a priest to please her and that she was not happy about the marriage. Unfortunately, a week later the new priest of the parish the groom had left read a letter from the bishop stating that the wedding was invalid in the eyes of the Church. Nevertheless, the couple have lived together in harmony these many years. They have two children, but the gossipers of the village were proved wrong when two years passed after the wedding before one of them was born.

Coming from a secular country, I was struck by the presence of young children and even babies at church services. If they cried or ran up and down the aisle, no one seemed disturbed. Religion and religious services were part of Mallorca, and almost everyone had a relative or friend who was a priest or nun.

After a first communion, the family had a celebratory "breakfast," in the old days at home, but as people became more prosperous, in a restaurant or café. If it took place at the home, there might be two sittings, depending on the number of guests. We, the foreigners, were always served first, a practice which obviously was meant as a token of respect but which I would have avoided if I could have. The food served consisted of hot chocolate, ice cream, *ensaimadas*, sweet buns and sweet champagne. (*Ensaimadas* can be plain or filled with cream or pumpkin jam for special occasions. The name comes from the word *saim* which means lard.) It was considered *comme il faut* to dunk the pastry into the chocolate, and some people wrapped pastries in napkins to take home for those who could not attend. At the end of the breakfast, the youngster for whom the affair was held was lifted onto the table and with sweeping gestures recited a piece of poetry memorized for the occasion.

No resident of the valley ever died in a Palma hospital, whether after an operation or as a result of serious illness. Sounds incredible and, of course, it is. In times gone by a tax was imposed on the movement of a corpse from one city or town to another, so the custom had developed, when a resident of one of the island towns or villages died in a Palma hospital (there were no hospitals except in the capital), to check the body out as though the person were still alive and bring it back home. The death certificate would show that the deceased had died at home.

Until the funeral, which took place within twenty-four hours of death, sometimes with a service at the home of the deceased, the coffin was open so that mourners could look at the body if they wished. Then they sat for a while with members of the family. The Mallorquíns are a practical people: If a death occurred in summer, two or three fans were set in motion in the room with the body. After the funeral the room was whitewashed.

When a man on our road died, Escha, as the next door neighbor, was expected to accompany the widow to the church so she did not go to the brief ceremony at the house beforehand. I did but certainly made a *faux pas* as I was still very much of a newcomer and had never been present at a local funeral. Knowing that usually people did not respect the exact hour for an event to begin, I went next door on the dot of 6:30 thinking I would be early, only to find everyone already assembled, the men in one room and the women in another. There was only one chair unoccupied, and it was in the front row so I had no choice. I was certainly a fish out of water as I did not know the proper responses as the service went on. When it came time for all the women to pass by the widow and express condolences, I had no idea of what to say so mumbled something unintelligible and left quickly. Some of the men then shouldered the casket and walked with it all the way to the church, followed by the others. The women stayed behind. I am not sure exactly what happened at the church, but the casket was immediately taken up to the cemetery for burial the next day. And that next day the widow and Escha and other friends and family members went to the church for a funeral mass. This event occurred some forty-six years ago.

A long time ago coffins were taken into the church for the service; but, I was told, due the occurrence of the bubonic plague (the Black Death) in the 19th Century, coffins were then carried rapidly to the cemetery for quick burial. Later on the authorities decided to keep coffins open at the cemetery for twenty-four hours to be sure that the person was really dead and not in a coma. I heard some stories which proved decisively the necessity of this delay. Some time during the 20th Century the Church officials made changes in the system regarding funerals, but nowadays again coffins holding the deceased go straight to the cemetery.   Incidentally, during my early years here, the cemetery had a separate section for any Protestant who was buried there.

Women all wore black at a funeral, and many middle-aged and older women never afterwards wore anything else. In the late 50's I once saw a twelve-year-old girl dressed completely in black – her mother had died but that still shook me.

The first time in my life that I saw a grown man cry in the flesh was in 1960, though I think most people have seen the famous picture of the Frenchman crying as the German forces marched down the Champs Elysees in 1940. The eighteen-year-old son of one of our neighbors had been hit by a car when he was on his motorcycle on the way to his job in the port. He was brought home and attended by a local doctor. We had no medical center in Sóller; but though the young man was not conscious, he was not immediately transported to a hospital in Palma. Later in the day he was taken there, but it was too late and he died that night. The next day I went to offer my condolences to the family. The father, in tears, was blaming the doctor for his son's death, and the doctor was not very successfully defending himself. As the boy had head injuries, it is possible that his life could not have been saved even with earlier specialist treatment, but I never trusted that doctor again. In fact, when I had had a very bad sore throat and needed medical attention, he had come to see me and amazed me as he barely removed the big cigar he was smoking from his mouth.

Although everyone was brought up as a Roman Catholic, almost no one seemed prejudiced against the foreigners who were not of their faith although it was assumed that we were all Christians. I do not know what reaction I would have received had I ever said I was, say, an agnostic, a Buddhist or an atheist. The Mallorquíns knew that we came from different backgrounds and had experienced a way of life that differed from theirs. There were, however, occasional exceptions to the general lack of prejudice. When Escha and I went to Ibiza in 1957, we did have an extraordinary experience with a young nun. An American tourist had joined us as we wandered around the cathedral and the surrounding grounds. As we approached a large building, the nun, perhaps a novice, came out of the door. Our companion greeted her in broken Spanish. She asked, "¿Es usted católico?"; and when he replied, "No, I am a Protestant," her face changed and she screamed, "Vete, vete." ["Go away, go away".] Escha thought she must be joking, but there was no mistaking the horror on her face.

The local people here were still prejudiced to some extent against the *Xuetas*, the converted Jews or, rather, the

110

descendants of the Jews who had converted to Catholicism hundreds of years ago during the Inquisition. Everyone in Mallorca knew who the *Xuetas* were, not by their religion, as they were all Catholics, but by their surnames, such as, Bonín, Picó, Valls, Cortés, Forteza, Pomar and a number of others. In Calle de la Luna in Sóller and Calle de la Platería in Palma the majority of the residents were *Xuetas*. In Fornalutx, however, for whatever reason, there are no Xueta names; and so far as I know, on mainland Spain there is no such category. The first permitted Jewish religious service in Spain in some 400 years took place in Madrid in the fall of 1959. I understand that two *guardias civiles* were present. The first full-time rabbi in this country was installed by the Palma de Mallorca community in December, 2003. A far cry from the massacre in 1391 of the Jews in Palma who were blamed by the populace for the plague that ravaged the island.

Incidentally, I had a student, a young man, who told me that he was not prejudiced against any nationality or race but then said that he would never marry a *Xueta* or someone from the mainland and certainly not a foreigner as "they were different from us." He subsequently married a Frenchwoman, and they have lived happily together for many years. I doubt that the *Xuetas* are in any way discriminated against nowadays.

Si Diós quiere ... y la Guardia Civil." That is a sentence we used to hear frequently. It means literally, "If God wishes ... and the Guardia Civil (also wishes)," and was used fairly casually, even automatically, after someone had said something like, "We expect to go to Madrid next week." But it is interesting that the name of God was linked with the power of the civil guard.

111

Gradually the second part of the sentence was dropped, and nowadays you do not hear even the first very often.

In the mid-50's a friend of mine had an experience which later made a good story. She was visiting the east coast of Spain and went one day with her baby to the beach which spread empty for miles. She was wearing a two-piece bathing suit and was dozing on the sand when suddenly she opened her eyes to see a *guardia civil* pointing his machinegun at her. He told she was indecently dressed and ordered her to accompany her. She pretended not to understand though his demand was obvious. Again and again he insisted and just as repeatedly she shook her head. Finally he looked around as though for reinforcements and finding none gave up and left.

On the other hand, we sometimes heard some terrible stories of the *Guardia Civil's* behaviour after the Civil War; but by the time I came to live here, though it was ever-present, it was not really intrusive except occasionally. We were careful never to criticize it or Franco publicly. My first contact with the *Guard*, not unpleasant, took place in 1959. In the fall of that year I applied for a residence permit, filling out and supplying the necessary forms. A *guardia civil* came to the house to interview me and ask for the same information I had already given. He was a nice middle-aged man, and Escha and I sat at a table with him sipping *coñac*. Somehow we got on the subject of divorce; and as I opened my mouth to voice my favorable views, Escha kicked me under the table. I managed to change the subject. After the man's departure, she said to me, "If you want a *residencia* you don't tell a civil guard that you approve of divorce, even a pleasant lowly ranked man like that."

The episode related above about my friend reminds me of the time years ago that I went topless at the beach in the Sóller port. Before I got back to my house in Fornalutx, an account of my action had circulated widely – it <u>is</u> a small village

Later I had a couple of experiences with them that might have ended with problems for me. Tofol told me one day that a *guardia civil* had asked him if I had pornography in my library. I am not sure what he told the *guardia*, but Tofol took no nonsense from anyone and probably laughed him out of the bar. On the other hand, I was somewhat concerned when a *guardia* came to me in the library and asked if it was *legalizada* and wanted to see my papers. I assured him that all was in order (though actually I wasn't really certain) but said that I kept all library documents at home. He then told me abruptly to bring them up to him at the *Guardia Civil* headquarters. I waited a few days, not wanting to give the impression that I was intimidated, and then went to the HQ with whatever official documents I had. The man fortunately was not there, and no one else had any idea about his inquiry or seemed interested. I left a message telling him that he could see me in the library when he wanted to. I never heard another word.

One day the *Guardia Civil* asked me to interpret as they were questioning a young American who had taken over as a squatter a vacant building in Deià whose owner had made a *denuncio*. Much as I disliked the idea of being involved, this was a request I could not turn down. The young man was being difficult and refusing to answer their questions, such as, "How long have you been here?" and "What is your home address?" and making nasty remarks about the officers in English. When they asked me what he said, I covered for him as much as I could while at the same time managing a warning word or two to him out of the side of my mouth. I think they knew that I was not translating everything he said, and he did not seem to understand that they could make life very difficult for him if he did not cooperate. He finally said that Robert Graves would vouch for him, but they did not seem impressed. Eventually the officers thanked me and took him off to Deià where he said he had hidden his passport. I never heard what happened to him, but the likelihood is that he was expelled from the country.

In addition to the lucrative contraband market in cigarettes and in medical drugs, attributed by everyone to the *Guardia Civil*, when you wanted a very popular but cheap cigarette lighter, you could not find it at the tobacconist's but generally bought it from the waiter at a café.

Many of the lowest-ranked *guardias* had little education even as late as the 70's. Two of them came to see me and ask all the same questions that I had answered on the application for renewal of my *residencia.* One of the questions was, "Where were you born?" *"En Nueva York."*

There was a pause and then one of them asked, "That's in England, isn't it?" I gasped "No," I corrected, "Está en los *Estados Unidos."* *"¿Cómo se escribe Estados Unidos?"* ["How do you write United States?"] Their ignorance truly seemed incredible.

In the 60's I had as a student a *guardia* who was a corporal but undoubtedly headed for promotion after he had finished a certain course of studies. He was well spoken and obviously of good family. We had many discussions about conditions and the government, and he was certainly open-minded. He told me that every Spaniard over the age of fourteen was required to have a national identity document and to carry it with him at all times. When I pointed out of the window to a man stripped to the waist who was working in the field and asked, "Even someone working like that?", he answered in the affirmative. And again he said yes when I asked if the law applied to someone at the beach in a bathing suit. He added that of course the force used its judgment and was sensible about carrying out the provision of the law.

At about that time a local classical music group to which I belonged, Juventudes Musicales, arranged a concert to take place in one of the hotels in the port. At the last minute the evening had to be cancelled as official permission had not come through. There was a law which prohibited meetings of any sort, whether educational, scientific, cultural or charitable, without previous permission from the authorities. I was told that this requirement included groups in private homes though I never heard of its being applied to anyone I knew. This law was not repealed until the post-Franco government came into power.

The civil guards could be unpleasant to the Mallorquíns, even without cause. When I decided to apply for a Spanish driver's license, I needed a good conduct certificate from the local *Guardia Civil* headquarters. The commanding officer was very polite to me; when I left his office, he bowed to me and kissed my hand. Waiting to see him was a cleancut young man with his hunting gun (guns had to be checked or registered annually). The officer turned to him and very sharply asked, "What do you want?"

With regard to the lack of schooling of the ordinary *guardia civil*, education for everyone did not get a boost until Felipe González became prime minister in 1982. Attendance at school before that was made compulsory in 1964 until the age of fourteen (prior to that it was up to the age of twelve), but these rules were not always observed. I had an eleven-year-old student for some four or five months who was working in his uncle's bar, presumably on a temporary basis. His uncle who was paying for the lessons wanted him to learn enough to be able to understand and communicate with his English customers, but the poor boy learned very little no matter how hard I tried to help him. My lessons were tailored specifically to his needs, but it was no use. After a few months, when I asked him, "What is your name?" I might get, "Eleven;" and after, "How old are you?" perhaps, "Very well, thank you." But he knew no Spanish grammar and had trouble conjugating the verb *ser* [to be]. After a few months the uncle, not unexpectedly, decided to terminate the lessons.

It was not surprising in such a poor country with inadequate educational opportunities for the majority that cultural activities for children were few and far between. Even colored pencils and crayons were in short supply and unknown to many. When Escha's grandchildren were here, they played with their neighbors. One day Katia, then seven, was with Paquita's sister, Catalina, who was nine. Both children were given paper and colored pencils. Katia, whose mother was a painter, knew immediately what she wanted to draw; paper and crayons were an ordinary part of her life. But the local child from a poor family had no idea what to do. She watched what Katia was doing for a few minutes and then hesitantly tried to copy her. It was incredible to us and saddening.

After I bought my house, I made a Spanish will and came across another indication of the lack of education of many people here. Before I signed the document, the notary read it to me but not only to me; I could not believe it when he said the three witnesses to my signature also had to listen to the reading. And not only that but the will contained a clause stating that I had given up my right to read the document myself. All of this, I presume, to avoid an illiterate person's pretending to read and then signing a will without full knowledge of its contents. That procedure has changed and the contents of one's will are now private.

The first person in Fornalutx to earn a university degree was Guillem in 1989. He later was my very good teacher of Mallorquín. Now there are some seven or eight others in the village who have obtained that level of education, chiefly women. Guillem has done what so many other Mallorquíns whom I know have done: Get a degree in one field, say, agronomy, and then end up running a hotel. In Guillem's case he did teach languages for a few years, but then he and his wife opened a restaurant in Sóller.

The National Institute of Statistics produced a report covering educational levels in Spain in 2002. Whereas 19% of the country's population over the age of sixteen had university degrees, in the Balearics the figure was only 14.5%. Of graduates nationwide, about fifty-nine per cent were women; but female students accounted for sixty-eight per cent of those who received degrees from the Universidad de los Baleares which was established in the 70's. For those "without studies" the figures were 14.4% national and 14.7% in the Balearics. Some four years ago the age for compulsory schooling was raised to sixteen years, but a new book written by Alvaro

Marchesis, who was Secretary of State for Education, points out that twenty-five per cent of Spanish pupils do not complete the required years. And in April, 2005, the law on education was changed for the fourth time since 1990, following a report that 21 per cent of fifteen-year-olds leave school without being able to read and write adequately.

Unfortunately, educating ones children wreaks havoc on many families' budgets. According to a report published in a Palma newspaper this year, it costs an average of the astounding sum of six hundred euros per child each year for books, uniforms and so forth.

Divorce, abortion – but I did know a gynecologist in Palma who secretly performed them -- and civil marriage only without a religious ceremony were not permitted under Franco, nor were contraceptives, known as *preservativos* (though they could be bought on the black market –- they must have been expensive as I heard of one woman who washed them for reuse). As a result, many couples had large families. A prize was actually given annually to the *familia más numerosa*, that is, the couple with the greatest number of children. The picture in the newspapers showed a wife and husband with sixteen or twenty or, at least once, twenty-four offspring. Horrendous. The only way these people could have survived was by living off their home grown produce, chickens, perhaps rabbits and a pig or so. And, of course, as each child reached twelve or a bit (or even much younger), she or he probably went out to work or assumed responsibilities for younger children or tasks on the family *finca*. Little by little, in spite of the Church's opposition to birth control, enormous families became the great exception.

A divorce law had been passed in 1931 during the Republic but rescinded eight years later, under Franco, which left some couples and children in an anomalous condition: People who had remarried were "living in sin", and children of those marriages were considered to be from the first marriage. Divorce was finally legalized in 1981, but there were certain limitations. For instance, a divorce could not be applied for until after the first year of marriage, and couples had to go through a legal separation and wait a year before applying for the actual decree. If after the separation, the wife and husband lived in different provinces, the divorce application had to be made where he had his residence. These and other requirements were modified or abolished in 2004 when the Socialist government came into office. For example, no reason now has to be given for suing for divorce. As the present Deputy Prime Minister, a woman, said, "No one has to justify himself/herself to get married, and no one should have to do it to get divorced." In 2003 seven out of ten applications for divorce were filed by women.

A young friend of mine, Margarita, asked if I would testify in connection with her petition for a legal separation and then divorce. She had lived here all her life and married on the island, but the groom was from the peninsula. The marriage was a failure from early on. The couple had gone to live in his mother's house in Catalonia. I had met her at the wedding and found her odd. She apparently ruled the roost, encouraged her son to lie around and not look for work and treated the young bride as though she were an interloper. About three months into the marriage, Margarita called her parents in great distress to say he had been violent toward her and thrown her out of the house. There was more than a suggestion that drugs were involved. Her parents rushed to the mainland and brought her home.

I was supposed to be able to testify to the following, as were the other three witnesses: That the young couple had lived on the island after the wedding (if not, the case would have had to go through the court in Catalonia), that I had seen the act (or acts) of violence and one or two other facts. I justified the first to myself because the couple had spent the first night of their marriage here and the second because I had seen Margarita's bruised face on her return from the mainland. The other three witnesses and I were called to Palma to give depositions, and eventually the decree came through, the husband not having responded in any way. Some time later she received her divorce papers which, incredible as the system may seem, had been sent directly to the local town hall to be registered and only then delivered to Margarita.

I developed a health problem evidenced by a few very painful attacks. One medical diagnosis led to another backed by x-rays which showed a gall bladder packed with small stones. I received a printed diet to follow for some months which wasn't difficult as it was similar to my usual diet, but what was amusing to me was the elimination of all alcohol except one glass of red wine with dinner. Apparently my Spanish doctor could not visualize a meal with no wine whatsoever. The doctor told me that if the stones did not dissipate by themselves, I should have to have the gall bladder removed. I stuck to a wineless diet for some months, but it did no good so I decided to have the operation in June, 1961. The day I went into the hospital I had to wait till evening to be operated on; and as I was not allowed anything to eat all day, I was not too pleased. (All my friends know that I enjoy my food!)   It was the custom, and still is to some extent, for each patient to be accompanied by a family member or intimate to give a hand when necessary. The nurses do the actual nursing: They give injections, change bed linen, put on dressings, but the accompanier helps the patient at mealtime or with such matters as personal hygiene, et cetera.

The hospital had no recovery room or intensive care section, so I was returned to my room after the operation where fortunately Escha was waiting. During the night I woke up and saw that the bottle containing the drip was empty. Escha, waking, saw it too and at once rang for a nurse. When she came in, she gasped, ran out and returned shortly with another bottle still in its wrapping which she removed with some difficulty. But she seemed not to know how to connect the drip, so Escha who had had some medical training did so.

I soon learned that there were no registered nurses on the staff -- or doctors for that matter. Nor was there a dietician. The hospital was staffed by nuns. I had to tell them that I could not eat the chocolate that was delivered to me for breakfast. One day my lunch consisted of meat, vegetable and potatoes, all breaded and fried. I scraped off the breading and wondered how other patients fared who might not know what they should not eat. Generally the nuns were pleasant and helpful, but they had not had much training. I asked the Mother Superior, a warm and lovely person, what happened in an emergency with no doctors in attendance. "Oh," she replied brightly, "we call your doctor and he comes in five minutes." Well, granted that there was little traffic in those days, I was glad that I never faced an emergency while in that hospital. I actually was kept in bed for seven days and in the hospital for three weeks.

My American insurance policy covered my suite which cost two hundred and forty pesetas daily, then about four dollars, and part of the surgical charges but not the eighty pesetas a day for Escha's meals. The surgeon, incidentally, had very kindly(?) saved the twenty-two stones he found in my gall bladder, so I faced them in a little jar when I first came out of the anesthesia!

In many parts of Spain and certainly in my area the incidence of gallstones is frequent due to the high level of calcium in the water.

Locally some of the doctors were good, some not so. During the 50's one came to Escha's house to give her an injection. She had her own needle which she had boiled beforehand. The doctor removed it from the hot water, *blew on it* and proceeded to use it on Escha. Another physician – the one who had visited me smoking a cigar -- gave a prescription to a friend of mine for a back problem without my friend's having to remove his shirt so the doctor could examine him.

All of that occurred years ago, however, and we now have very fine and well equipped hospitals and well trained doctors and nurses. In fact, the British National Health Service sends teams over to recruit medical personnel for their institutions. In recent years I have had a hip replacement and two cataract operations, the first done privately so as not to have to wait too long and the others by the Social Security system, and I have no complaints about the medical or nursing care. Not so long ago a survey of one hundred and twenty-six national health and twenty-nine private hospitals showed that the government hospital in Manacor on this island is among the top such institutions in Spain.

I would now not hesitate to have any medical problem cared for in Spain. An amusing sidelight concerns the hip operation which was covered by my own insurance though it did not include the cost of the prosthesis. On the fourth or fifth day after the operation, a man came to see me in my room, presented me with the bill for the prosthesis and asked for payment. I was incredulous as naturally I had expected to pay when I left the hospital. I certainly did not have the pesetas with me or my checkbook. Fortunately my good friend Micky was there at the time and, able to lend me the money, wrote out a cheque then and there. I always wondered whether the man would have asked to have the prosthesis back if I had refused to, or could not, pay his bill.

Incidentally, it is somewhat unusual to see a patient alone in a doctor's office, unless to pick up a prescription or for a minor complaint, as everyone is generally accompanied by a family member or intimate friend. In the 50's and 60's many people, particularly men, were reluctant to visit doctors and especially dentists. My Sóller dentist told me that he had had a patient whose mouth was in such dreadful condition that he asked the man when he had last brushed his teeth. The patient looked puzzled and answered, "Never." The dentist told him to go out, buy a toothbrush, use it well and then come back. Dentistry here, by the way, was a specialty of medicine but now is a five-year course in its own right.

After I had been here a couple of years, it became apparent

that Villa Rua was not large enough to accommodate Escha's writing and musical activities and my students who came and went during the day, so I advertised for an apartment or house. In September, 1961, I was lucky to be offered a six-room garden flat halfway between Villa Rua and the center of town, called Ca'n Bessó. It was spacious for one person. One of its features was a tiny room off the entrance hall where a student who came early for a lesson could wait. As at Villa Rua, the bathroom water was heated by the *económica*. There was a large plot of uncultivated land around the house, which I was free to use. The owner, Juan, asked one thousand pesetas (now six euros) a month. I offered him nine hundred with a lump sum in advance for the first six months, and he agreed. The flat was unfurnished and I still had to watch expenditures, so I gathered up furniture and odds and ends here and there. One day I arrived on my bicycle with some bricks and then brought in two long smooth boards I had ordered. My landlord appeared very puzzled and asked what on earth I planned to do with them. "I am making shelves for all my books." Juan looked really disgusted but with a, *"Cada uno a su gusto"* ["Everyone to his own taste"], he walked away. Foreigners were certainly peculiar people as no Mallorquín would be caught dead with such makeshift kind of furniture.

Americans are considered to be very materialistic, but it seemed as though Mallorquíns were also. Juan's daughter who was about twenty-six years old had been engaged for seven years, and she and her fiancé had still not fixed a date for their marriage. When I asked her about it, she replied that they had not yet bought everything to set up housekeeping, and that included a dozen of four or five different kinds of glasses, at least twelve monogrammed sheets and pillowcases, complete furnishings for every room and so on. When I pointed out the joy a young married couple would have in planning and saving for various additions to their home, she said, "Yes, but suppose I become pregnant or there is an accident or illness and one of has to give up working?" That is the thinking which produces the answer, "Very well <u>for the moment</u>," in answer to the question, "How are you?"

Many Mallorquíns were also too proud to buy anything secondhand. I myself during those first years here was earning very little and, reasonable though life was, could not afford to buy new clothes. My mother occasionally sent me a box of clothes – generally used in good condition but occasionally new – and after I had made my selection, I offered them to friends who were pleased to accept them. A few years ago a young Englishman married to a local woman complained to me that his wife would not permit him to buy clothes for their two children at a bazaar or charity shop even though children's new clothes are very expensive here.

One day I offered a pair of men's shoes which had been worn only once by a friend of mine to the woman who cleaned my house in Sóller, for her husband. She was deeply offended. And I made a bad mistake when a local friend of mine asked whether I might have anything to contribute to a bazaar the alumnae of her school were arranging. I offered some English books which she said they would be happy to have; but when I went to the affair, I was embarrassed to see my offering in a corner because they were used books from my library whereas everything else on sale was brand new.

At Ca'n Bessó in the kitchen there was a well which supplied me with drinking water. The town running water was not really bad and could be used for cooking, but it was not advisable to drink it. My landlord kept a pig, some years two, in a pen on his land back of my house. Every day I fed whatever leftovers or garbage I had to the animal(s), and everything was gratefully accepted. The *económica* produced hot water for the kitchen though, as at Villa Rua, I did not want to light it except perhaps once a week. When cool weather arrived and I wished to shower in hot water, I realized that the water heated by the *económica* cooled down by the time it reached the bathroom as the pipe from the tank in the kitchen went up through the roof and over the full length of the house before it came down to the shower. When I offered to pay half the cost of a small electric water heater, Juan agreed to install one, then decided to pay the entire cost but, "Don't tell my wife."

My electricity meter indicated that I could use a maximum of 1,940 watts which seemed sufficient to me at first as, besides the water heater, I had only the radio which I seldom used, light bulbs and an electric blanket with transformer. Later I bought a refrigerator and then a toaster, so I had to be careful not to have everything in use at the same time.

The only form of heat was the fireplace in the livingroom, but it did not draw very well. When Juan had added the apartment above, he had connected the fireplace upstairs to my chimney, as a result of which neither worked properly. To encourage the fire, I used a *bufador,* a long thin metal tube, which I directed at the flames and blew into. One day I came home to find my livingroom full of flying bees and they were still coming in from the chimney. I was told the only way to get rid of them was to build a fire of straw in the fireplace and smoke them out. This I did and was lucky not to get stung before they all left.

As the fireplace did not heat the room sufficiently, I bought

126

one of the first butane gas heaters which made the room liveable in cold weather. The problem with the use of this heater was the occasional shortage of the small blue bottles of gas. One cold winter the store was frequently out of them, and when new lots came in there were only fifty. I would race up to the shop and stand in line, hoping to be in time for one of them..

The rest of the flat was another story. One night when the temperature in some of my rooms was 48 degrees F (9C), I slept with my clothes for the next day in the bed and dressed under the covers the next morning. On the other hand, when I returned from my first visit to the U.S in the summer of 1962, everything I had left in the third bedroom with the door closed was covered in mold.

One morning at Ca'n Bessó when I went out to the pigpen, I noticed something curious poking its head up through the earth along the path. It looked like a stalk of asparagus, and a day or so later that is what it proved to be. Then a second came up, followed by a third. In fact, over a period of a couple of weeks, some ten or twelve fat asparagus spears appeared, but unfortunately only two or at most three were ripe at the same time. My landlord professed ignorance about them, but he told me he had had English tenants before who must have planted them. They came up for a few more years but then died off.

Another year I carried back from America a very fine bunch of growing chives with roots and earth. The minute I arrived I planted them in a big open space where I thought they would thrive. Unfortunately, Juan was not familiar with chives; and one day when I went to cut some, I could not find them. They had been buried under a load of dirt he had just had delivered

– he thought they were weeds.

After one visit to the U.S. I brought back seed of some very good corn on the cob as Juan had told me I could plant whatever I wanted on part of his land. In those days corn was not available here for human consumption or, probably, in many other parts of Europe. I watered my corn assiduously, bought fertilizer for it and daily examined every plant for signs of health and growth. Finally the corn came up, not so high as it ought to have but with good-sized ears. I could hardly wait to try it but first offered my landlord a few.

"*No, no, señora, graciás.*" I understood: His father had never eaten corn, his grandfather had never eaten corn, no one he knew had ever eaten corn, and he was not going to be the first one to do so. Of course, the corn he knew was for animals, and he could not understand that mine was different. Most Mallorquíns were loathe to try any unknown food. I saw an example of this just a few years ago when a Sóller supermarket had okra on sale, the first time I had seen it here. I was eager to have some but was leaving the island that day for a couple of weeks so did not buy any. On my return I went back to the store but, alas, the okra was gone and has never been on sale there since.

Another example of the difference in eating habits between Americans and Spaniards was illustrated some thirty or forty years ago when Hamburger Heaven, one of the first restaurants of this type in New York, opened a branch in Madrid. The first day many *Madrileños* went to see what this new and original counter-eating place was offering. When the hamburgers were placed before them, they sat looking puzzled, then asked for knives and forks, not imagining that they were supposed to eat with their fingers. The next day each customer had a full set of cutlery.

I never felt insecure living alone in Can Bessó though one or two odd things happened after I had been there a few years. For example, a pair of socks disappeared off the clothes line overnight, and one evening I was reading in my livingroom when I heard the kitchen open and then close (I almost never locked it). I hate to admit it, but I did not have the guts to go see who was outside. One morning the drawer of my little table outside the kitchen was open, and the few cigarettes I had purposely left in it were missing. So I set up a trap with a cord across the garden path attached over a branch to a large can. I went to bed that winter night with my coat on the bed and a large flashlight handy. Suddenly I heard the can bang and I screamed out something (but in my fright, in English), jumped out of bed and raced outdoors. I saw no one and again I lacked the courage to look into the outside laundry room. The next morning I called the Civil Guard; they investigated and found that a man in the neighbourhood, mentally disturbed but harmless, was the culprit. He never came back, but I believe the poor fellow was shortly afterwards sent to a mental home.

My landlord was like some other people who always made me repeat what I said in Spanish (though with others I held long conversations without any problem). When I greeted him in the morning with a *"Buenos días, Juan,"* he invariably replied, *¿Cómo?"* ["What?"] Surely even though I spoke with an accent, he could have understood, "Good morning, Juan."

My mother's first visit to me took place in 1968 when she was 85 years old. She was agreeably surprised by my home which by then was fairly comfortable, by local standards. I guess she had thought that because I lacked lots of the gadgets and equipment found in most American homes and had to dispose of my garbage to the pig, I lived under almost slum conditions. (Some years ago the government issued a rule prohibiting the feeding of food refuse to pigs.)

Earlier I mentioned monogrammed bed linens, and it was surprising that so many people of low incomes had monogrammed shirts and other items of clothing. There was almost no ready-to-wear; dresses, jackets, shirts, trousers and so on, as well as sheets and pillowcases, were all made by hand. I have always preferred casual dress, so I wore *alpargatos* almost all the time; but when the young women of the community dressed up, in spite of the rough lanes and roads, they wore high-heeled shoes, the type which I had worn in New York but happily given up here.

On Sunday mornings many men, in corduroy jackets and trousers and with berets on their heads, congregated in the main square of Sóller for both social and business reasons. They drank a *palo con sifón* or a *vermut* or a *coñac* while they chatted, negotiated a sale or discussed crops. If there were any women, they were never alone but always in two's or three's. Even in summer women did not wear sleeveless dresses. German tourists, the men, were the first to wear shorts in town, and that caused some eyebrow-lifting. Young couples were accompanied by a younger sister or brother - undoubtedly, chaperonage had been more strict years before. Many people went to the Bar Willy after mass for hot chocolate and *ensaimadas* or *croquetas* which I thought were made of chicken. When I discovered that they were made of bull's testicles, I almost had a heart attack; but as they were delicious, I got over my shock and distaste at the idea and continued to eat them.

Many years later the building in which the Bar Willy was located collapsed, and extraordinarily enough, the inhabitants upstairs were given sufficient warning by the nervous barking of their dog to rush out before the edifice came down.

The weekend showings at the two movie houses in Sóller were very popular as although TV was available on the island and had come to Sóller in 1951, no one I knew had a set. Too expensive for most people. (One man who could afford a set very kindly placed it facing the street and often left the door open; the neighbors brought chairs and sat in the street enjoying whatever program was being presented.) When television sets became generally available, they proved to be a godsend to those who were not great readers. (I did not have a TV until some time in the 70's.) If an American movie was shown, it was frequently not the complete version as there was heavy censorship, not only on films but also on all printed matter. Newspapers could not report, for example, the death by drowning of a tourist or other disaster that occurred on the island. In April, 1966, however, a law was passed which, in the words of Manuel Fraga Iribarne, Minister for Information and Tourism, was "a compromise between total freedom and complete state control, neither of which is desirable." I think, however, state control was uppermost. For example, Charlie Chaplin's movie, "The Dictator," was banned all during the Franco regime, and he did not die until the 20th of November, 1975.

In spite of the fact that censorship was softened in many

areas, as late as 1980 – and I quote from a local newspaper – "The editor of one of Spain's leading independent newspapers was given a three months suspended sentence and fined fifty thousand pesetas for an article saying that a recent prison sentence on the editor of a girlie magazine for publishing nude photographs was a violation of the freedom of expression guaranteed in Spain's new constitution."

One week in the early 60's Sóller was abuzz with the fact that the band of one of the ships of the United States' Sixth Fleet, which was visiting Palma, would be performing locally. A group of us attended and were thrilled with the performance. The band was completely professional, and undoubtedly few *Sollerenses* had ever heard such fine live music. The first half of the program was given over to jazz; the second half, to rock 'n' roll. I was eager to hear the latter as even though it had come on the scene in the late 50's while I still lived in New York, I had never listened to it. I have to admit that I was caught by the rhythm. The rest of the large audience was obviously equally enthralled at the quality of the music.

Sitting immediately in front of me was Margarita Servera Colom. Hers was an interesting story. Born in Brooklyn, daughter of a doctor who had emigrated from Sóller, she had visited the island a few times when young. She was here when the *Movimiento* [Spanish Civil War] began and she stayed on and married. When I met her, she was concerned about her American passport which had expired, because she had property or investments in the States and thought she might have to go back one day. I encouraged her to see the American consular agent in Palma, and she finally did and got her new passport.

When the program ended that night and we all started to leave, the band began to play "The Star-Spangled Banner." Margarita stopped dead. "I haven't heard that played in thirty years," she said as tears formed in her eyes. I was moved by her emotions.

Mention of the U.S. Navy brings up the time a friend of ours, Escha and I entertained a sailor on his one-day shore leave (the Sixth Fleet made regular visits to Palma). He was a pleasant and well mannered young man, and we enjoyed having him. I could hardly believe it, though, when he said that the ride from Palma to Sóller was a novelty to him as he had never before been on a train. He was a Texan and was accustomed to travelling by car or plane.

The United States had no consular office on the island, so that during the 50's if an American wanted to renew his passport or conduct other such business, it was necessary to go to Barcelona. Then for a couple of years the consul came over to Mallorca for a one-day visit four times a year, and finally in the early 60's a consular agent, a Mallorquín, was appointed who is still acting for the United States. Unfortunately, a good part of his time and energy has been devoted to clearing up problems caused by some American sailors who, when their ships come into port, try to drink up all the alcoholic beverages they find.

In the neighborhoods and small villages in the evenings when all the daily tasks were finished, the women sat outdoors in good weather facing their front doors while they talked or knitted or did other such work, the men having gone to the cafés. Even in winter women did the family laundry outdoors at the public washhouses where the water rushing down from the mountains ran cold all the time, the first person to come choosing the spot nearest to the flow of clean water, the second next to her, the third further along, and so on. Nowadays the houses all have running water, and many have washing machines so it is not often that you see anyone laundering outdoors. The lanes and pavements in front of houses were swept and cleaned every day by the women, and the children on the way to school were always immaculate.

An annual job for the women was the whitewashing of the interior walls of their houses, and they were very skillful at this. It was definitely not considered work for a man. In 1960 to *blanquear* [whitewash] the entire house cost us 310 pesetas, some five dollars at that time.

Not many people had telephones as the exchange in Sóller at first had only one plug board with one hundred and fifty lines. In the early 60's Escha applied for a phone, and so did I as I was now living at Ca'n Bessó. As there were no lines available, we had to wait almost four years until a third position plug board was installed. Her number was 423 and mine, 360. The year after I moved to Fornalutx dial phones came in. Until then the local operator would take a message for you if you were not at home. She also frequently listened in; and if there was a pause in the conversation when, say, one of the speakers was looking for some information, she would interject, "*¿Hablan?*" ["Are you speaking?"], and you would have to make sure she did not cut the call off. The last four digits of the six of my number were 1972 which were easy to remember, as the dial phone system was installed in that year. Many people were hesitant to use the phone or seemed a bit afraid of it. In the 70's I took up an offer from Telefónica to install an answerphone. A day or so later I came home to find an almost hysterical message from Francisca who looked after one of "my" houses. She obviously had not understood my recorded message in both English and Spanish and was upset to hear "voices" on my phone.

Now and again I heard some odd comments from American or British visitors, and as a resident I resented criticisms of the Mallorquíns and their (and, in some cases, my) way of life. One woman living here criticized the people because their houses had no doorbells! She made other critical remarks until I was annoyed enough to ask, "If you were living in your home state of Tennessee, what would you say to Spaniards who were critical of the American way of life? Wouldn't you say, 'If you don't like it here, why don't you go back to Spain?'" She had the grace to reply affirmatively, so I pushed on, "Well, why don't you go back to Tennessee?" She did a little while later.

Also, "How odd that they don't advise you personally when a certain tax is due," or "What a funny combination of names, Batle Batle." (The word *batle* in Mallorquín means "mayor," and some years ago the Sóller mayor's last name was Batle.) My response to this comment was, "And if John Major had been a major in the British army, he would have been Major Major."

A visitor said, "How strange it is to see women carrying babies in their arms."

I was puzzled. "How else would you carry them?"

"In a baby carriage, of course." I was appalled - appalled

at myself for having forgotten about such an ordinary thing in America which was almost unknown here. These days parents spend a fortune on some of the models on sale.

It was difficult for Americans in their conspicuous consumption society to understand that we lived without all the equipment, manufactured goods and entertainments available in the United States. When some of them did appear in the shops, they were pricey. I returned to the United States in the 60's for the first time after some years here and had to ask my brother in whose new house I was staying how to turn on the faucets in the bathroom; I had never seen such modern equipment. The hot running water thrilled me and I could hardly wait to get into a shower after my arrival. But after visiting friends over a period of weeks, I was shocked at the wastefulness of almost everyone. Things were discarded that I would have given my eye teeth for in Sóller. Nonetheless, I had no desire to return to live in the United States; and when I was asked, at least once every visit there, "Aren't you homesick for America?" I was vehemently tactless in my reply.

During one holiday when I was with my mother in Maine, we were invited to have dinner with friends of hers who were interested in my life in Spain and asked me many questions. I told them that I did not have a TV set, and that though I had a radio the reception in the valley was not very good. They knew I was not a bridge player. At the time I was teaching thirty-five to forty hours a week, running my lending library and doing some interpreting jobs. So when they asked me what I did for amusement, I was momentarily taken aback as I had very little free time. What *did* we do for amusement? I answered that I read tremendously – one year some eighty books – and occasionally in summer I got to the beach. I added, "We have drinks parties and converse." (This conversation took place some years before I resumed playing tennis.) There was a brief silence, and I felt that I was a social failure. Perhaps I should mention that my life was not typical of how most of the foreigners lived then; they were painters, writers or musicians or, more often, retirees with no special occupation.

In the 60's, 70's and 80's numerous large properties in the valley were acquired by foreigners who had the funds necessary to modernize the buildings and produce beautiful gardens. Many were the big parties we enjoyed on these *fincas*; in those days most of the foreigners knew one another. Of course, one of the places where newcomers became acquainted with older residents and came for information was in my library.

Chiefly in summers a lot of my English friends and a few from America came to enjoy their holiday homes, so there was a lot of social life. At least once a summer a large group of us went to have dinner at *Cal Dimoni* [House of the Devil] in Algaida. This was a wonderful place with its huge charcoal-fired grill in one corner, in addition to its standard kitchen. The menu was not enormous, and we always started with their excellent *sopas mallorquines*; the portions were so generous that if there were twenty of us, we ordered for, say, fifteen people –- and each of us had two servings. Then there were grilled chops, steaks and two or three kinds of sausages plus salad. At the end the waiters put one or two bottles of *hierbas* on the table; and it was my custom, as the arranger of the evening, to take home what remained. Alas, the restaurant changed as did the foreign colony, and we do not go to *Cal Dimoni* any more.

One year I had a cast on my leg and was using a crutch,

having severely torn a tendon in my right ankle when I stepped on a ball during a tennis game. The friend who was taking me home from the Algaida restaurant dropped me off at the foot of the many steps leading up to my house from the main road because I assured her, with bravado, that it was not necessary for her to make the difficult maneuver with her car to reach my door. She therefore left. I had a large bag full of mail that a friend had picked up for me from the post office, a half bottle of *hierbas*, my handbag and the crutch – and the street lights had already been turned off. I tried a step or so and thought, "I just can't do it." But as I obviously could not stand there all night and there was no one else around, I sat down and worked my way up backwards step by step, hoping the bottle would not slip out of my hands. I must have looked mad as a hatter, but I finally reached the top and my door. I knew another time I would not be so damned independent.

As for other possible social activities, there was The British Club in Palma which finally decided Americans were acceptable and changed its name to The British American Club. As a courtesy, I joined but as I almost never took advantage of its facilities, I withdrew after a year. The club disbanded a few years ago because of lack of support.

One diversion which was not available to most Mallorquíns was tennis as in our area, at least, there were no public courts or club then. When I was sixty-five I bought a tennis racquet and began practicing wherever I could, but after a thirty-or-more-year lapse I never got back the skill I had once had. A few of us did play regularly for a time, and now there is quite a lot of interest among the local young people and public courts are available. It has helped to have two Mallorquíns, Carlos Moyà and Rafael Nadal, among the top tennis players in the world.

I admit to spending many hours looking at tennis matches on TV, and years ago I used to go to London in late June in order to see Wimbledon on friends' TV. Now we get coverage on digital TV.

A popular sport here is the use of the slingshot which is not surprising inasmuch as the Balearic Islands were famous for their stone slingers as far back as two thousand years ago. The slingers carried three slings wrapped round their heads, one for long shots, one for medium distances and the other for close targets. Caesar employed slingers from these islands in the Gallic Wars, and Hannibal found them better than archers in demolishing an enemy. The Greek word *ballein* means "to throw," and the historian Polybius stated that this was the origin of the name of the islands.

I was invited to the wedding of Gilberto, a young man whose father Escha and I knew well. Tony did not seem to have any particular work, but he did a variety of jobs for us and was very helpful. He used to ride around in a small wagon drawn by a mule. His son, however, who started out working on building sites, was ambitious and set up his own business as a constructor. I referred an English couple to him, his first foreign clients, who were very satisfied with his renovation of the old house they had purchased. From than on Gilberto's fortunes prospered. Incidentally, this couple had been the proprietors of the famous Treetops Hotel in Kenya where the present Queen of England was visiting when she learned of the death of her father and so ascended to the throne.

Weddings for most of the local people took place in late

morning, but Gilberto and his *novia* [fiancée] decided on a more formal 6 p.m. ceremony, at which he wore a tuxedo. After the service while the couple and their witnesses were signing papers, all of the guests went on to the reception and dinner at the Restaurant Atalaya in the port, very up-market at the time. Waiters walked around with trays of assorted drinks, and people were in a happy mood by the time the newlyweds arrived. I happened to be standing near the door as they opened it, but they did not enter. They seemed frozen and unable to move. The guests also quieted down. No one moved – it was for only a few seconds but seemed much longer - so though I was embarrassed to call attention to myself, I stepped forward and gently guided them into the room. Then everyone relaxed, many came forward to embrace the new couple, and the festivities continued – in fact, until well after midnight.

MY OWN HOME

In the late 1960's Rosa and Carla bought a little house in Fornalutx, which needed a lot of work to make it habitable, after which they hoped to install a kiln for Rosa and perhaps open a small art gallery. They urged me to buy the adjoining larger house, Ca Mestre Cinto. The two houses were interlocking and had been part of a *casa señorial* [manor house] a long time ago, three hundred to five hundred years, at least. I had never considered owning property here and actually had little money to make a purchase. The price was very low, though, as the house was a complete ruin. In fact, when the mother of an American friend of mine, a woman who lived very comfortably in California, saw the house and went inside (though there was no way of getting upstairs), she told her son that I was crazy as "There is no way Elena can make a livable dwelling of it." I am glad that I did not hear that, and she was certainly wrong.

Incidentally, I never considered changing the name of the house as I felt that would be a slap in the face of the family which had previously owned it. And I was delighted when an elderly neighbor came by shortly after I moved in and told me she had been born in what was now my home. Her son who lives in France drops in to see me on the rare occasions that he is visiting Fornalutx.

At any rate, I paid the initial fifty thousand pesetas and sent for the balance from the United States, the final payment to be made in three months' time when the seller and I would sign the deed. As it happened, the Sóller notary was away on holiday with no replacement on the fixed date. No matter, the seller was not anxious nor was I – business matters could be quite informal at times. When the notary returned, we both went to his office in the summer of 1969, I paid what I owed to the seller, we signed and that was that.

I have to admit that I did not check very carefully the description of my house before I signed as I knew it had been copied from the seller's deed, and the notary said the deed was in order. What I did not pay immediate attention to was the fact that the cellar of my house was not mentioned. The village at that time had no sewage system, and the question of ownership of my cellar arose when Rosa, Carla and I agreed to install a septic tank in it which would serve their house as well as mine. As mine was higher up than theirs, the cellar was on a level with their ground floor, and there was a door in the wall between the two houses. As good friends, we did not bother signing a document covering this joint ownership and the fact that the cellar belonged to me. When they sold their house, however, even though the buyers were friends also, we all deemed it prudent to cover joint ownership and responsibility of the septic tank and my ownership of the cellar in a private agreement; and when they sold later on another agreement was signed by the new owners. I once asked the notary's assistant if he thought I would ever have any difficulty proving ownership of the cellar, and he replied, "Oh, no, what's under your house is yours." This, of course, is not always true and certainly not in a village with houses one after the other up a hillside. My lackadaisical attitude about the omission of mention of the cellar in my deed proved to be a mistake, as I learned thirty-five years later when I had to pay for the official papers to register the inclusion of the cellar.

There was an unpleasant postscript in connection with the purchase, though nothing to do with the seller. I had dealt all along, except for actually paying the money, with the owner's brother-in-law as she, a widow, was oldfashioned and not accustomed to handling financial matters. One day after I became the owner of Ca Mestre Cinto, this man accosted me in the bank and asked me why I had not paid him his commission. I was astounded. After all, he had represented the seller and if any commission was to have been paid, surely she would have been the one to pay though probably, it seemed to me, not to her own brother-in-law. He began to attack me, "You have lived here long enough to know that the seller pays two per cent and the buyer one per cent." I knew no such thing but learned later that that had been the custom earlier but had more or less fallen out of use. I was furious at him and while still in the bank thrust some bills at him with a loud retort. Of course, he could not accept money shoved at him in that manner in public so he refused it. Afterwards I gave the matter some thought: He was well known in Fornalutx and some of the foreigners thought highly of him and were grateful for his help as he took care of many of their problems. I was a newcomer to the village, although known by many people, so I finally decided to pay him his one per cent which was a very small amount and keep peace in the family. Incidentally, his local nickname could be translated into "slippery."

I had doubts about my ability to reconstruct Ca Mestre Cinto as I knew little about the technicalities of house renovation and had never been a property owner. Both Rosa and Escha, who had recently moved to Fornalutx, had urged me to buy and had promised to help me. But good friends though they were, their assistance was minimal, and I frequently had to make decisions without knowing what I was doing. At any rate, Rosa never had her kiln or art gallery, but I did end up with a home which I love. I was lucky to buy then because although at that time there were many ruined or rundown properties on the market, the supply has dried up in recent years. And those which remain are ridiculously priced.

I chose Gilberto, who was making a name for himself, as my builder. He got the town hall permission and paid on my behalf the required two per cent of the one hundred thousand pesetas that he declared the work would cost. Even with the low materials and labor costs of that era, it was obvious that the rebuilding would amount to much more than that figure. But the estimate was in line with the custom according to which no one ever declared a real price or cost. Nonetheless, one evening when I was in Fornalutx a man from the local town hall delivered a notice to me (how he knew I was there I did not know but in a small village everyone seems to know everything about everyone else). This document stated that the estimate for new construction had obviously not been correct (at this point I was almost afraid to read on, thinking that I would be required to tear down what had already been built), that the total cost would probably rise to two hundred thousand pesetas – which was considerably less than the real figure -- and therefore I was told that I had to pay an additional two thousand pesetas for building permission. I was so relieved I could barely wait until the following morning to rush to the town hall with that sum in my little hot hand.

Gilberto was a constructor but not a general contractor, i.e., he did not take on the responsibility for the electrical, plumbing or carpentry work, so it was up to me to employ whomever I wanted and usually to track them down when necessary. Of course, they all knew each other and worked together. I had expected that Gilberto would give my work his personal attention -- after all, I had given him a leg up a few years before – but it did not work out exactly that way. While he showed up occasionally, he put his younger brother in charge whom I liked but who was not very experienced. I was not bothered that only a couple of men usually worked at any one time on the house as I was not in a hurry to move from Sóller to Fornalutx. Nonetheless, when Gilberto explained that he had to take the men off my work for a few weeks or so as he had a deadline on a big job in the port and those weeks turned out to last five months, I was not too pleased.

During that five-month period, I did not visit my house. When I did, I was horrified to see that the view of the valley from my livingroom was blocked by some new construction on the top of the neighboring house which had been bought as an investment by a German woman I considered a friend of mine. The work presumably had town hall permission, but I was dumbfounded that she had not advised me of her plan to add a roof terrace and, if possible, find a way that would affect my view the least. I spoke to her about it, but she brushed me off. The same person a little while later cheated me - I use the verb deliberately -- out of a commission on a sale on which I had done all the preliminary work until she intervened. That caused the end of our friendship, and I later learned that I was only one of many others who had suffered from her sharp practices.

Nonetheless, the view from my roof terrace cannot be spoiled and is so breathtaking that I often remind myself not to take for granted the splendor of our impressive mountains.

As I was very occupied with classes and my library, during the rebuilding I could spare only short visits to the house. Often neither Gilberto nor his brother was on the site. There were no plans of the house, and we had no architect or draftsman, so one of the men would ask me how I wanted something done – this way or that? How high did I want the windowsills? A door to open from the left or the right? One window or two in the lower bedroom? Gilberto made drawings on the rough walls, but the workmen did not always follow them. There were a couple of marvellously curved walls, and I just stopped the workers in time from evening them out. They looked at me incredulously, then shrugged.

That reminds me of an old house in a neighboring village which a friend of mine was renovating and which had an enormous rock protruding into what was to become her diningroom. The workmen were considering how to destroy and remove the boulder when she fortunately arrived on the scene to insist on their leaving it as it was. Again I am sure they thought, "Another crazy foreigner."

One feature of my house which pleased me very much was the *cisterna* [cistern] under the *entrada* [entrance hall or room]. It was full of water but certainly not clean as rain had been flowing in from the roof for many years with no control over its cleanliness. In days gone by before the house fell into disrepair, many of the neighbors used to get their supply of water from this cistern. For some months there had been gypsies living in a part of the house though there was no plumbing --- their sanitary arrangements had been incredible --- and there were only a few light bulbs hanging from the ceilings to give illumination.

A pump was installed and it took a day and a half to empty the cistern which is very large. Then I was asked to buy four bottles of ordinary vinegar, and with these two of the workers went down into the cistern with rags, sloshed the liquid around and after clambering out pronounced it clean. (After they came up, one of them swore he'd never do such a job again underneath a house as he suffered from claustrophobia.) I was taken aback as it seemed obvious that there would still be a question of the water's quality. Shortly afterwards a small van brought a quantity of water but I waited for the first heavy rainfalls to clean the roof before I removed the new thick cork which had closed the entry to the cistern and let the clean water rush down into it. I repeated this a few times during that first winter until the *cisterna* was quite full. Only then did I begin to use the water. It wasn't that Fornalutx did not have running water by then, but it was full of calcium which coated the lead pipes and the kettle. I used the cistern water for tea, coffee and ice cubes and also drank it on the few occasions that I imbibed that liquid, and I still do.

The very old wooden beams, splendidly crooked and irregular, in the *entrada* and what was to be my bedroom were still in good enough condition to be kept. Unfortunately, the new floor above the *entrada* proved to be too heavy and six of the old beams had to be replaced some thirteen years later. The bedroom beams were sturdier and they remain.

When it came time to take the old roof off the open attic room which was to become my livingroom, birds were nesting on the beams; obviously they did this annually. I told the men they could not disturb the birds and would have to work elsewhere in the house until the eggs were hatched. In the same room I planned to have a good fireplace, English style, not a large Mallorquín one which did not seem to give out much heat as most of it went up the chimney. One of the men was to go to Rosa and Carla's house to get the measurements of theirs of English design. I was, therefore, very unhappy one day when I got to the house, having missed a couple of days, to find a small, inadequate fireplace half built. The men said they had already spent a day and a half on it, so I very reluctantly agreed to let it stand. By the time I got down to Sóller on my Mobylette, however, I knew that I could not live with it. Back up I went and told the men to tear it down and redo it. Of course, they said they would but begged me not to tell their boss. There were many other difficulties of this sort, and work proceeded slowly; but I had told the builder that I was not in a hurry to move to Fornalutx, thinking that when I did, I would lose a number of my students who had no method of transport up from Sóller.

There were a couple of amusing episodes during the work on my house. The carpenter's son, Pep, only eighteen but very tall, installed a dish drying rack in the kitchen. When I saw it, I did not know whether to laugh or cry as I should have needed a ladder to put any dish into it, Pep being some thirteen inches taller than I. Another time he affixed some hinges to which I paid no attention, but one of my students told me that nails instead of screws had been used. The next day I casually mentioned this fact to Pep, and he told someone that I was very clever to have noticed this.

I wanted to deepen some shelves on one side of the kitchen, but I did not know how far my house extended and Rosa and

Carla's began. I checked with them. Rosa said, "Dig through as far as you want, and if you don't break into our house, the space is yours." Rather informal but that's how matters were often resolved in those days.

In the summer of 1971 I went to the United States to visit my family and to ship some furnishings from my mother's house in Maine over to Fornalutx. We put the oriental rugs into waterproof bags and then sewed them into burlap and packed my English bone china and other breakables in barrels. These were sent to the shipping company in Brooklyn for transshipment to Palma de Mallorca and delivery to the house. Alas, nothing went as promised and paid for. The ship docked at Barcelona, and my things were put into storage. I received a bill covering delivery from there to here. While charges mounted, I protested to Barcelona and to Brooklyn and got nowhere. I even went to Barcelona for a day to get my stuff out of storage and on the way, to no avail. Finally I had no choice but to pay the extra amount, and eventually the shipment reached me with a few things either missing or broken.

The big day in my life when I would move into the first home I had ever owned arrived: the 13th of October, 1971. Friends had helped me move small pieces, but for the larger ones, suitcases, et cetera, I employed Big Benito from Fornalutx who had a small truck. (There was also a Little Benito, a distant cousin.) He was alone but was very strong so could handle everything himself. The only problem was the diningroom table which he could not get around the top of the stairway. Instead he stood on the back of his truck, raised the table in both arms and was about to shove it across the cement windowsill into the room when I grabbed a couple of rags and covered the sill, thus saving me a refinishing job on the table.

In Sóller I had had only a shower, so I was looking forward that first night to a full hot bath and then to my new (well, actually old but new to me) bed with new sheets and new pajamas. I turned on the hot water for the bath. Not a drop. I turned on the cold water. Not a drop. So I went to bed unwashed and disappointed. The next morning I roared down to the plumber's and raised hell. He sent a man immediately: Result, someone had forgotten to turn on the water supply for the house, and I was still ignorant of how things worked in my new home.

Incidentally, when the plumber's final bill was presented (at his request I had paid him a good sum earlier), I found a number of discrepancies so asked him to come to check them out with me. I asked him a second time, then a third, but he did not show up. Months passed and I honestly forgot about the outstanding bill which was relatively small. The plumber never spoke to me about it nor did he come to the house, and the whole matter slipped my mind. Years later I came across the bill but by then the plumber had retired. I let the matter drop because I believed that he had recognized that his bill was not correct.

The crowning moment took place a month later in November of 1971, when I had a housewarming for Ca Mestre Cinto. More than forty friends celebrated with me. Alas, of that number not one is still on the island and, in fact, only one or two may still be in the land of the living.

PROPERTY MANAGEMENT

My real estate and management business kept me extremely busy, and I also still had my lending library. For the latter it was not only a matter of being open a couple of hours a day but also all the work I had to do at home. .Nonetheless, I enjoyed my full life and my contacts with a variety of people though some of my book borrowers (and stealers) left me incredulous or amazed, especially the few people who actually thought I should supply books free of charge "just like the public libraries." And in connection with my property work I had a vast number of experiences which kept me hopping and sometimes guessing about the mental processes of other people. But more important were the close friendships which developed during the years.

Before I opened my lending library, many of the English-speaking colony met most mornings at the Bar Royal in the square of Sóller. Pep, the proprietor, was a fine-looking, sturdy man who never bothered with a jacket or sweater in winter, walking around with his shirt sleeves rolled up. We all liked him but were not so fond of his companion, Marga, who worked very hard in the bar but was very jealous. She may have had her reasons because he obviously was very fond of women, all women, and flirted with them. It all seemed quite innocent to me, but eventually it turned out that Marga was being deceived by the one woman of whom she was apparently not jealous.

Maggie and Harry Brownell were an English couple who bought and renovated an old house. She was a skilled gardener and also kept some beautiful birds in big specially constructed cages. Harry and Maggie would regularly drive up to the Bar Royal, open the trunk of the car and watch as Marga and sometimes Pep lugged out and loaded cases of wine and other items which they had ordered. They all seemed to be very friendly. Harry must have been dozing or occupied in some way when Maggie and Pep met privately. Or perhaps he knew and did not care.

One of the first and certainly the biggest property I managed, Son Roqueta in Sóller, led to very good friendships with the two couples who owned it, but I did work hard for them. When at their request I checked their deeds I found out something curious about their right to irrigation water. Water rights are very valuable, and the system used here is hundreds of years old. The water for a finca may arrive at any hour, for example, at 10:38 at night or 3:27 in the morning. My friends thought they *owned* forty-five minutes weekly of irrigation water; but when I examined their deeds and other papers, I found the language to be murky and it appeared that they paid annually for the water (like a rental) which came into their storage tank from someone else's spring and also paid something to the waterman who weekly supervised the receipt of the water. This man also saw to the actual irrigation of the trees, moving tiles which blocked the channels and replacing them after each tree had received enough water.

My people asked me to buy half an hour's water weekly for

them, and it took me two years to persuade the owner of the spring at the top of the mountain to sell it to them. After I had signed the deed for the water, the owners congratulated me for the accomplishment but immediately asked me to negotiate for another fifteen minutes. This time I got the water fairly promptly but at a rate four times higher than the first allotment. It was most fortunate for that *finca* that they had been able to buy their own supply as, oddly enough, the intermediaries who had been supplying water originally cut it off soon afterwards, claiming that they needed it for themselves.

Friends of the owners and others often came out to stay on the property, sometimes arriving late at night or over a weekend. I met them and saw them installed, introduced Francisca who took care of the housekeeping to them and generally made them at home. Francisca, a good cook, always had a welcoming meal waiting for the guests.

Fred, the member of the family with whom I chiefly dealt, sometimes asked me to take on responsibilities which I felt were not within my province, but he always accepted my decision when I pointed out that I could not undertake them. He was also very kind to me over the years, and he made accommodation available to me in London for many of my holidays there. In fact, I had a wonderful relationship with every member of both owner families. When at sixty-five I decided to retire (though I never did completely), it was a sad parting although we are still in close touch.

I was the agent in the sale of a property up the steps in Fornalutx. One of the owners, Bert, came with his companion and her son to stay one summer; and when he left before they did, he gave me a sizeable amount to cover the final cleaning and laundry for Cruz as she took care of those jobs. After the companion and child had gone, Cruz went up to the house and found every sheet, blanket, towel on the floor or under the beds so every piece had to be laundered, and the refrigerator literally full of growing plant-life.

She had to make twelve trips down to the collection point with the garbage, bottles and other refuse. The money left by Bert was therefore not sufficient, and I paid Cruz the small difference. A month or so later I visited London and was invited to dinner by Bert and his friend. I drew him aside to explain when she came along in time to hear that he still owed me a little money. I was embarrassed when she exclaimed that she had left the house in perfect order. Bert paid me the sum due but he looked a bit dubious; she, I think, honestly believed what she said.

After Paul Krakozci received the deed of sale to his grandfather's house, he put it on the market. I showed it to the sister of a friend of mine, Katrina, who decided to buy it with some money she had just inherited. She made this decision, however, just an hour or so before she had to leave for the airport. There was no time to go to the notary, so I drew up a contract, known as a private agreement, which was legal but could not be registered. (The deed of sale would be signed after payment was made.) I was able to sign on behalf of Paul as I held his power of attorney. Since both Paul and Katrina lived in London, we arranged that she would deposit the purchase money before a certain date in my account in London, for which I gave Paul my cheque. It seems a bit complicated but at the time there was a good reason for this way of handling things. I then wrote to my bank manager explaining the circumstances so that Paul would experience no difficulty in withdrawing such a large sum of money. The manager seemed almost unwilling to allow the transaction, but it did go through without a hitch. My account looked healthier than it ever had for a short time but, alas, after the withdrawal it returned to its usual low balance.

In 1973 I came across two little adjoining houses in Sóller, each with a small garden, which were urgently for sale as the owner was ill in France and needed funds. I had a good prospect for each house, one of whom promised to send funds to cover the price as soon as he returned to London, and we shook hands on the deal. There was a delay in the receipt of the money; and the owner's representative warned me that if the owner died before papers were signed, there would be complications for any possible buyer. I therefore took a flyer and for the first time in my life borrowed money from a bank and bought the two houses myself. Unfortunately both deals fell through so I was stuck with the loan and the interest on it. Eventually I got rid of both houses and paid off the loan but I barely covered myself on the sales. That taught me a lesson about verbal contracts.

I represented a charming American ballet dancer who bought a house at the end of the village. This was another case of an absentee seller who had a representative here. The house in question had a small garden and was part of a bigger property, so for the purposes of the new deed the notary had to know how many square meters were involved. The old man representing the seller had no idea, so I measured the oddly shaped garden by walking foot in front of foot and then adding a bit for the tree and a small piece of land to one side. When the deed was prepared it said "three hundred and eighty-five square meters or *lo que sea*" ["whatever it may be"].

Josh, who became my neighbor in Fornalutx, did me a rather bad turn although he probably did not realize it at the time. We were in correspondence for some months regarding his retirement plans before he left the United States, and I found a house for him to rent here. His arrival coincided with my vacation off the island, so I did not meet him until my return. As he had told me he wanted to buy a property, I had one or two in mind for him. To my dismay he had not waited for my return but had gone directly to the owner of the house next door which was for sale and signed a contract with her, thus eliminating any possibility of a commission for me. I did not sell many properties but the commissions were what put the jam on my bread – teaching and the library certainly did not.

Some newcomers soon learned how to fit in, and many artists, writers and musicians produced some fine work here. On the other hand, other foreigners could not cope with a different way of life or their funds ran out. Josh, an amateur painter, enjoyed his life here for a while and was entranced by the scenery and the light, but he returned to the United States because he found most of us too liberal for his taste. Some of us women actually wore slacks, and we were opposed to Nixon!

There was another artist we came to know who lived with his family for a year or so in Sóller. He produced overwhelming black structures which none of us liked but which seemed to satisfy him. In fact, he was so self-satisfied that he was not very popular. One day he stated that he felt his art was the most important area of his life, that if he had to make a choice, his wife and children would come second. They soon moved on and he was not missed.

Rosa, Carla and I decided in 1973 to dip into the real estate market. Our first venture was the purchase of an old and rather odd house in Fornalutx, narrow but quite high. Because of Rosa's background and ability to handle tools, she and Carla would do as much renovation work as they could. I would handle all the legal and official paper work and hire the workmen needed. From our point of view the purchase went well, but there was an interesting sidelight: The seller, a Frenchwoman, apparently intended to leave the country without paying a commission to María, the intermediary, and also planned to carry the cash with her without declaring it or requesting permission -- at that time there were restrictions concerning the sums that could be taken out of the country. She had reckoned, however, without María's unwillingness to be done out of what was due her. She said to the Frenchwoman, "All right, don't pay me anything but see what happens when you get to the border after I advise the officials what you are carrying with you." The Frenchwoman paid up.

We sold the house with its furnishings to some Swiss people after we had done some work on it   In this case there was an unpleasant episode when the buyer accused us of having removed a blanket! Since then this house has changed hands twice, with the price increasing considerably each time.

In 1975 we jointly bought a lovely rustic house with many fruit trees on its half acre of land. The house needed renovation, a part of which my two friends were able to do themselves. As usual, I hired the craftsmen, handled the paper work and was the official buyer. Had I not owned a house already, I should have liked to keep the property for myself. It took a couple of years to find a buyer. Mrs. Francis, who lived in England, paid a deposit and after she obtained the necessary military permission which foreigners were required to have in order to purchase rustic properties, she was prepared to pay the balance of the purchase price. The fun then began. Her English lawyers would not agree to release the money until I signed the deed of sale here, and I would not sign until the payment was made. Through a fluke it all worked out. The cheque had been made out, but Mrs. Francis' accountant in England had been instructed not to send it until the lawyers gave the okay. One day she went into his office when he was not there, saw the cheque, popped it into an envelope and sent it to me. I then of course signed the deed, but what her lawyers' reactions were I do not know. We had a very pleasant relationship with Mrs. Francis in the years that followed.

Two of the most disappointing experiences in my real estate activities occurred very shortly after I began in September, 1971, to advertise in the literary/cultural American magazine, "Saturday Review". My advertisement was worded: "AMERICAN, living, working Majorca, will find you living quarters. Davis, Sóller, Majorca, Spain " (There was no other Davis in Sóller though, surprisingly, at one time there were five of us in Fornalutx.) I ran this ad a number of times over the years, and it had a fairly good response. The actual financial result, however, was meagre. The very first insertion brought an inquiry from a retired dentist in Kentucky. I replied fully, he answered with more questions. After my reply to him he seemed to be on the point of arranging his and his wife's visit for one or two months in 1972, so I eagerly awaited his next letter. When I had not received one, I wrote to him again early in February. I was truly puzzled and disappointed never to have an answer or to hear another word from him.

A second prospect behaved much worse. In his case he

had given me his arrival date, so I booked a hotel room for a few days and lined up one or two houses as possibles for him to rent. He and his wife never arrived, nor did he afterwards ever communicate with me in any way. Perhaps I was naïve, but I could not understand such behavior.

As both of these disappointments took place at the beginning of my advertising venture, I considered giving it up, but fortunately I persisted and as the years passed many pleasant relationships resulted. One letter really made me raise an eyebrow, though. A young woman wrote from California asking for information but added, "If you are middle-aged or older, don't bother to reply …" I did not bother!

Then there was the Pennsylvania man who wrote a rather odd first letter, some of which I could not understand. He replied to my response saying that he would arrive to "your home," and added that he wanted a "studio with good piano" and among other things, "Need your Girl Friday typing etc. services … Will want models of your knowledge." There was more of the same. He then said he was paralyzed and would require a full-time masseur. I suspected from his address that he lived in an institution and wrote him a discouraging letter. Seven months later another long, unbelievable letter arrived from this man, evidence of a very disturbed mind, so I immediately returned the small check he had sent and told him that I was "absolutely unable to supply even a small proportion of your many requirements." I did not hear from him again, *graciás a Diós.*

One day just after I had moved to Fornalutx, a woman with whom I had corresponded called me from Palma as her cruise ship was making a one-day stop there. She told me that a friend of her husband's cousin's son-in-law's butcher's wife (well, that is an exaggeration but it was a complicated link) knew someone by the name of Ferguson who had a house in Sóller. I thought I knew all the Americans in the area, but I did not recognize the name. Where was the house? She said the house was called Villa Rua and it was in the section known as La Huerta. I was astounded as it had, of course, been my home for my first two and a half years here. Shortly after this telephone call I received a letter from a Larry Ferguson, introducing himself and his family, and that was the beginning of what developed into a long and close friendship between all of his family and me.

Some years later the Fergusons discovered an oddity about their ownership of Villa Rua when they were in the process of selling it. The deed described the plot but made no mention of the house on it – this was actually not unusual. When Larry learned about this, he applied for a correct *escritura* which came through in time for the sale of the property

An American law professor who had a house in Fornalutx made a proposal to me one day. Years before they had bought a small plot overlooking the sea which they now wanted to build on. There were complications, however: They did not have a registered deed of sale for the land, nor had the German woman from whom they had bought though no one was contesting their ownership. The plot was in an area with its own problems regarding legality. In addition, there was some question as to whether the plot met the requirements for size in order to construct on it.

What the Ruperts wanted me to do was get their papers in order –- and there was a possibility I could do so after considerable time and effort. Then I should have plans for a house drawn up and approved and supervise the entire project until it was finished when I was to sell it. The Ruperts would send funds regularly to cover the costs involved. When I had disposed of the property and paid all the bills, then – and only then – would I receive any compensation: half of the profits.

It looked like a good deal for them. True they would bear all the expense, but I would do all the work, sign all the papers and carry the full responsibility over what might turn out to be a long period before I received a penny. I turned down the proposal.

Perhaps the longest–running relationship with a prospective buyer concerned Boris' little house before it was sold to Katrina. Through friends two Belgian women came to see me in 1978 about their desire to purchase a house in Fornalutx. I showed them eight or more possibilities, and they finally decided on Boris' though it was not yet on the market; he was ill in London and obviously would never return to the village. The house became available after Paul inherited it. The two Belgians and I corresponded until August, 1983 – there were finally twenty-three letters between us as they raised question after question. It turned out to be a lot of wasted effort: they never replied to my last letter nor did they ever buy anything in Fornalutx.

The most sensible act by newcomers, in my estimation, was carried out by friends in Deià. The day after Dick and his wife moved into their new house, they went to the local town hall, introduced themselves and asked what taxes and other charges they would be responsible for. The official to whom they spoke was overwhelmed as never before had a foreigner made such a request. Most new home owners here seem to feel that it is up to the governmental agencies to find and notify them of their responsibilities.

PERSONALITIES

One of the interesting things about a place like Sóller or Fornalutx is that many people of very different backgrounds and interests are drawn together simply because they share the same nationality or language. So many of my friends and acquaintances here I'd never have met if we all lived in a big city like London or New York.

While most of the foreigners resident in the valley were British, French, German or Belgian, many other nationalities were represented. When I had my right leg in a plaster cast in the 70's because of a torn tendon, caused by my stepping on a tennis ball, I asked everyone I knew to write a comment or sign the cast. Eventually there were a dozen languages, including Hungarian, Russian and even Hebrew and Korean. But today, in 2006, that number of nationalities is nothing compared with the almost 155 who live and/or work in Palma though thirty are represented by only once, two or three people.

The oldest foreign resident in Fornalutx and one of the most interesting was George Manipoli. Mani, as he was known to everyone, had come on the ferry from Barcelona one day in the 1920's and made his way up to our village. He was so entranced by it that he bought a house for fifty pounds. Needless, to say it was not endowed with any modern conveniences –- I don't suppose many houses in Fornalutx were –- and, in fact, it was only in the 70's that hot running water reached the upper floors of his house. Before that Mani's faithful and hardworking María daily had to carry buckets of hot water upstairs for his bath. Mani, having sung in the opera chorus in London, had many musical friends who came out from time to time. It was always a pleasure to be invited to lunch or dinner at his house when he had visitors.

Mani bought a few other ruins which he renovated for the use of his family and friends. The Town Hall held him in high regard or were in awe of him; when he complained that his daily siesta was spoiled by the village children's noise, they passed an ordinance in 1970 prohibiting under-fourteen-year-olds to play outdoors between two and four p.m. Needless to say, this rule was repealed a long time ago.

Mani developed arthritis so badly that he could hardly move, and finally María could no long take care of him. His closest niece came and urged him to return to England where he would receive the care he needed. He resisted for a while, but he recognized that he had not long to live so he would call his neighbor across the road, who loved music, and declare that he would not last the night out and she could take all his great records, which she did. The following morning, when he woke to find himself still alive, he would demand that she return them. This happened two or three times. He did finally leave, but after a few weeks he died. His ashes were returned to Fornalutx where the priest was at first reluctant to conduct a funeral, probably because he had never faced such a situation. The family prevailed on him to do so, and a nephew carried the urn with the ashes to the cemetery where Mani was laid to rest in the village which he had loved.

Brucey was a Scottish bachelor who had spent his professional life working for a British bank in South America. He was bright and had attained a moderately high rank but got no further because, according to the standards of those days, he did not come of a "good" background. In addition, he was very rigid and very tough on those who did not toe the line; one very hot day long before they had airconditioning, he told me, one of his staff had come to work in an open-neck shirt without a tie, and Brucey discharged him on the spot. He did not seem to recognize my distaste at his action. Brucey had settled here in the 60's and followed a completely unnecessary daily schedule: Up with the alarm clock at 8 a.m., drinks in the square of Sóller, then back to his rented flat for more or less the same lunch every day. The woman who took care of him usually bought the identical ingredients daily to simplify her life; and as Brucey was a creature of habit, he paid little attention to his food. Every day he noted in a little book every peseta he or she on his behalf spent, not that he was pressed for money or stingy in any way. He liked his friends to join him at his table in the square but was very annoyed and not above showing it if someone he did not care much for asked, "Mind if I join you?" and sat down. One of his quirks was that he would not stand up if a woman friend stopped by his table and stood chatting for a few minutes as, he said, the Mallorquín men did not do so.

He would not admit to it but I think Brucey was a bit lonely. Cathy, an English friend of his, used to lunch with him a number of times a week, and I tried to do so frequently. There were some subjects on which we agreed, but I always froze when he began on his feeling that the police forces were right, no matter what they did. And there was no way you could convince him to follow his doctor's orders to cut down on salt, for instance, when he began to have circulatory problems in his legs, even when he began to have trouble maintaining his balance. Eventually he was in such a bad state that I called the British Consul (Cathy was off the island) who told me that he had thousands of people in the Balearic Islands for whom he had responsibilities and if Brucey had any family at all, he himself could do nothing. There was an 80-year-old brother living in Scotland, so he came down to accompany Brucey to London where a great-nephew was to meet him and take him to a nursing home in the south. We had a few difficult moments the day he was to leave Sóller as the brother had mistakenly given Brucey a sleeping pill that very morning. When I arrived, he was sound asleep in a chair. We opened windows and slapped his cheeks until he was partially awake. We then located two men in the street below who kindly helped to carry him down to the taxi. He lasted only a few months in England as I imagine he missed his life in Spain and had lost interest in living. I settled all his affairs here but was surprised and of course delighted to learn that I had been left one thousand pounds by the old boy.

Snobs can be found everywhere, of course, and we had a few. One English woman, Sally, was proud of her ancestor who had led one of the Crusades though she never referred to the fact that he was also known for his cruelty. Oddly enough, it was only in the year 2001 that the city of Leicester in England renounced a ban on Jews that had been put into effect by this man 800 years earlier. At any rate, one winter Sally and an Australian friend, Norma, gave a dinner party in the latter's house on New Year's Eve. The women guests were asked to wear dinner gowns and the men, tuxedos. The women probably had no difficulty in complying, but only three of the eight men had such formal clothes here. At the end of the meal the "ladies" withdrew and left the "gentlemen" to their port and cigars! You have to keep in mind that at that time many houses in Fornalutx had no running water or indoor plumbing, the method of heating was fairly primitive and the steps and village streets very rough.

Sally, by the way, later told an American friend the reason that the largest aircraft carrier in the world, part of the United States Sixth Fleet at that time, could not enter the inner bay of Palma was due to the admiral's insufficient seamanship!! He was devastated but anyone who has seen that bay would know that no large warship could be accommodated in it.

The wife of one of my English friends told someone she did not think much of me because I worked for a living!!!! And one English couple whom I liked in spite of their being very conservative had a big party and did not invite the only black American living in the community – my friendship for them cooled rapidly after that. At that party the host toasted the "English" Queen. And that did it for the Australians present.

There was the Lavender Woman - we called her that as no one ever saw her in any other color. In fact, she appeared to wear the same outfit always though it may not have been so. She lived in the hamlet of Binibassi and although she was very pleasant, she did not socialize much with any of us. We knew very little about her though naturally there was plenty of speculation about her life – some of the foreigners seemed to have nothing better to do than gossip. One day we realized that she had gone without telling anyone of her plans, and no one ever heard a word from or about her again.

Pauline Corinth owned the Hotel Sol Playa in the port of Sóller where many of us used to meet. She had had a conventional upbringing in England and was well educated; she spoke at least four languages and her mother, seven or eight. Pauline had been presented at court as a debutante. After that she had apparently flung conventionality to the winds. She was a big outgoing woman. In contrast, her companion Antonio was small and quiet. Together they managed the hotel which was usually full of English people who enjoyed a good time. Still, the staff were taken aback one day when the elevator door on the ground floor opened to reveal Pauline stark naked and laughing like a fool. She did take a drink or two.

One evening she and Antonio came to have drinks with Escha and me. The conversation became animated, and soon the exchanges were in three or four languages. Suddenly, Pauline picked up her companion, hugged and kissed him and exclaimed, "I love this little man!" He looked too dazed to reply.

She told us some wonderful stories of her escapades. She tried to bring a load of Swiss watches from the European mainland into England. The crane which was moving cars onto the ferry almost buckled when it tried to lift Pauline's car off the ground, and the port officials rightly became suspicious: All of the tires proved to be packed with watches! Either this time or another she ended up in an open prison and, having been put in charge of the gardens, began selling off the plants – at least, that is what she told us.

She wrote and published a book about her life, which terrified Antonio as in it she described certain of their illegal activities in Spain. Although his last name was not mentioned, the book included a very clear photo of him; and he feared a visit from the *Guardia Civil*. They did come calling one day but on Pauline as the book was too indiscreet in its language about the Spanish government, as a result of which she was expelled from Spain for a year or so. On her return she toned down her way of life until she gave up the hotel (Antonio having returned to his wife), moved to another part of the island and then back to England with her younger English companion, where she died a couple of years ago.

Pauline's book was one of the most popular in my library. I had two copies but unfortunately both of them disappeared, probably not returned by people who then left the island.

I spoke of snobs earlier and we also had foreign residents who, shall we say, doctored their previous experiences. One Norwegian told us he had been a nuclear scientist though his vocabulary and conversation did not seem to represent someone with that background. Nonetheless we had no real reason to doubt him until one day someone casually asked him something about Nils Bohrs, the famous Danish physicist in the field of nuclear science. Said our man, "Who is Nils Bohrs?" That cooked his goose.

And then there was Gudie, a Swedish artist, who was believed to have been the mistress of one of the Scandinavian kings. And the amateur potter who was a grandson of an ex-president of the United States. And the Englishwoman who decorated her newly renovated house by gluing tufts of cotton on the walls of the livingroom. And South African Beatrice who was having an affair with a well known Spanish writer who was violent; she used to show Escha her bruises, and she told me they showed how much she loved him!!! She also suffered financially as her small pension was sent from a bank in her country to her account here, and she had to accept the official rate of exchange - most of us, of course, changed money on the black market. Beatrice went to live in the south of Spain, had emotional problems and, alas, committed suicide.

The Swiss artist Marianne had kicked up her heels in North Africa before coming to Mallorca and continued a rather wild night life that caused some raised eyebrows. She was, however, a magnificent painter of flora and was painting meticulously over a period of many years every flower and plant that grew on the island. Unfortunately she had very little money and her little home, more or less a shack, offered her few comforts. She did not complain, though. It was always amusing to have a conversation with Marianne as she spoke rapidly in a mixture of French, Spanish, Mallorquín and perhaps a few words of some other language thrown in for good measure.

And there were many others. Mollie Craig and her husband had bought a house here in 1931, and therefore she considered herself the leader of the foreign residents. She had a young grandson who showed talent as a ballet dancer, but she discouraged him as she thought all males in this field were homosexuals. And there was the Rhodesian (before the country changed its name) who had obviously retired to the island because of its cheap booze. His only "conversation" seemed to consist of, "Sit down, have a drink."

Trevor Sanderson was a person of some standing in England, but he had beautiful manners and never threw his weight around. Our backgrounds were completely dissimilar, but we got on well together and I always enjoyed his company on his visits to Sóller. He and his wife Betsy bought a large old house with ample land in the valley. Though it was to be only a holiday home, they renovated and furnished it lavishly in the English style. For example, Betsy bought luxurious material in London for the curtains. The garden was her delight and she spent a fortune and long hours to bring it to perfection. Their marriage foundered, however, partially because, as Trevor told me later, he had wanted to live simply here in rustic surroundings whereas Betsy had preferred a more formal and lavish life. When they separated and decided to sell, she gave him her power of attorney for her half and he gave me his for the entire property.

An Austrian bought the *finca,* paying the full price, and we both signed the private contract; the deed of sale could not be signed until military permission was received. (This permission was never granted to foreigners to buy within a certain number of meters of the coast, and there were other restrictions. These laws were eliminated some years ago.) Stefan went off to the Middle East where he had business connections. When the military permission came through and Stefan returned, I assumed he would sign the deed, but he did not before he left. This sort of thing went on for a couple of years. The next time I saw him, I warned him that I was getting on in years and should anything happen to me before he had his *escritura* or to either Betsy or Trevor, who were now divorced, he would have great difficulty in getting a deed. So on his next visit I finally got him to the notary's. Just before we signed, the notary turned to me and remarked that my power of attorney was now some years old. "I assume Mr. Sanderson is still alive?" Of course, if he had not been, it would no longer have been valid. I answered truthfully that I had had a Christmas card from him some months before. That satisfied the notary. I had not lied to him, but I had not added that just a few weeks before I had been advised of Trevor's death. The notary's chief clerk told me later that when a power of attorney was not recent, the authorities sometimes checked on its validity, but fortunately in this case they did not. I have to add that Stefan presented me with a cuckoo clock which I installed in my diningroom. Unfortunately I generally forgot to wind it, and it never worked well so I gave it to someone else.

Pete, a friend of mine, sold his house because he wanted a larger one. The buyer was a Mallorquín who was married to an Englishwoman and lived and worked in England. As Pete had to return to the United States, it was arranged that the buyer would send the next payment to his sister, a neighbour of Pete's, who would turn it over to me for deposit in Pete's account here. When the check arrived the sister, Catalina Bernat, advised me and we met in the bank. "There is a slight problem," she said. Her brother had asked his young daughter, born and brought up in England, to pick up a cashier's check from his bank and send it to her Aunt Catalina. But the daughter made two mistakes: The check should have been made payable to Pete; and knowing nothing of Spanish customs, the daughter thought her aunt was called Catalina Colom as her husband was Pedro Colom. So the check was made out in a name which was not correct, and Catalina could not endorse it.

"*No se preocupe*" ["Don't worry"], she said to me. It just happened that she had a cousin whose name was Catalina Colom and ... Just then the cousin entered the bank. Without introducing us, my Catalina handed the check to her cousin who endorsed it and walked out. Catalina gave it to me and left. Surprisingly, the bank accepted it for credit to Pete's account. Nowadays such a situation could not be resolved so easily.

172

One sale of a house I made in August, 1975, had a curious ending. John A Chillworth, but known as Andy from his middle name, was interested in a small ruin which he wanted to renovate as a holiday home. He decided against buying as his wife was afraid of flying – they lived in England. Nevertheless, the morning of the day of their departure, he showed up at my house, saying, "I want to buy anyway." There was no time to go to the notary's office, so I typed up a private agreement, based on copies of others in my files, and we went to see the seller. I lent Andy fifth thousand pesetas for the down payment – no risk to me as he worked for the British Government, and I knew his boss who had a house here.

Andy returned my outlay and made full payment for the property. On his one visit back here, I introduced him to two friends who were available to help him with the renovation. I explained to him the necessity to obtain military permission and told him what papers he should supply and how to go about it Andy gave me a power of attorney to deal with the red tape in his absence. No papers were forthcoming from Andy though I wrote to him three times. Finally I heard that he had moved and had not received my letters. In the meantime I learned from his boss that he had a reputation for starting projects which he never finished. The last letter I sent to him was quite strong as he had not reimbursed me or others for various outlays for which he was responsible. He never replied directly but sent to me through his boss a check which covered the expenditures.

One day out of the blue I received a letter from an English bank unknown to me stating that they had been requested by their client, Mr. John A. Chillworth, to send me a reference. They added that they were unable to send such a reference to a private individual and asked for information on the situation.

I was briefly puzzled, then realized who their client was and understood that Andy had confused the instructions I had given him years before with regard to obtaining military permission. Obviously, it was not to me that the reference and other papers were to be sent, but Andy never did follow through.

The property remained registered in the seller's name, and she paid the small annual taxes on it for a few years until I advised her to let them go. When she died some years later, her French step-children who were the heirs probably knew nothing of the sale to Andy. He never showed up again, and the property was finally sold a few years ago to someone else. So Andy lost his entire investment, and I never heard another word from him.

The Gordons were a soft-spoken Australian couple. He had been a bank manager in a small town but had had to retire for health reasons, and she was a painter. They loved children but had lost, so I understood, their only child many years before. One day they "borrowed" Escha's young grandson for lunch, and Bradley took the boy off through the fields to their house. The youngster picked up a bird's feather which he was admiring, but Bradley took it from him, threw it away and rushed him into the house to wash his hands. When I heard about the episode I could not believe it until I saw that Bradley was a frequent hand washer. When the Gordons came into the library one morning and invited me to have *ensaimadas* and coffee with them, I told them I could eat only one of the two they offered me, but I soon saw why we each had two. Bradley asked for a knife and carefully sliced off the top of his and discarded it and the outer ring. I looked at him in puzzlement. He said, "There was a fly in the bakery." "Aren't there flies in Australia?" "Of course, but we have screens."

He came into the library frequently and always went into the men's lavatory immediately to wash his hands. When I jokingly chided him for taking his basket in with him every time, he then used to leave it next to his chair. And whose basket was stolen one day? Yes, Bradley's.

Unfortunately, many people had a dream of coming to live in what they thought was the paradise of Mallorca, often with no knowledge of actual year-round living conditions and/or with insufficient financial means. There have been a number of British couples, some with children, with little or no experience in the restaurant field, fascinated by the idea of working and living on an island with sunny weather twelve months of the year (which we do not have) who have bought a *chiringuito* [beach snackbar] or restaurant in Sóller or the port and then lost their shirts a few months or a year later. Usually they spoke no Spanish and certainly not Mallorquín, and they knew little of the legal and tax requirements involved in running a business. Also they did not realize that there is a tourist season here, and in winter the port and beach are almost without any activity. One couple with four young children found themselves in desperate straits when the tourists disappeared in late fall their first year as proprietors of a snackbar in the port. The children would literally have gone hungry if some of the English residents had not fed them. The family soon left the country.

Another unfortunate was an American woman, María, who had lived in neighboring Deià some thirty years ago and who arrived in Sóller with five million or six million pesetas – this was just before the euro became our official currency. Her fund - six million pesetas would amount to approximately $32,000 or £23,000 -- was absolutely insufficient to purchase even a tiny cottage at the time of her arrival, she apparently not having given any thought to the increase in prices over a thirty-year period.

María told me she was estranged from her family and had been mistreated by the social services people in New York. She arrived at a holiday time when most of the hotels were quite full, but her main difficulty in finding accommodation was due to her unkempt and almost dirty appearance. She was dressed inappropriately and seemed never to change her clothes. Time and again after spending four or five days in one hotel or *hostal,* she was told the room was no longer available. As a courtesy the Red Cross allowed her to leave her suitcases in their reception room; but when she came for clothes, she left the suitcases open with items hanging out onto the floor. The Red Cross found her a room in a home of some sort, but she would not accept it, perhaps with reason. She continually begged everyone she met for help. As a newcomer and not from a European Union country, she was not eligible for assistance from any governmental agency. The American consular agent in Palma told her she was illegally in Spain and should return to the United States. She said to me, "Never will I do that. I'll destroy my passport first."

During one week or so she wrote me illegible letters every day. I felt guilty that I had no way of helping her. She was well educated and intelligent but obviously in need of the kind of help not available to her here. Eventually she moved to another part of the island and, I heard, asked for assistance from many other people. I had forgotten about her when last year she called me with another appeal and said that this was the last time she would bother me. Again there was nothing I could do, much to my own distress. There seemed to be no agency or group which could or would help her.

Another American woman's story ended in a true tragedy. I first met Vicki when she rented a small neighboring house in Fornalutx. She was a painter and a very good cook; she was also a very good drinker but not uncontrolled – at first. She was fun and we all enjoyed her company. One June she and I gave a drinks party at my place to celebrate her birthday and Escha's. But as time went on her personality began to change and she became quarrelsome. Even our very good priest got fed up with her, and one night when she woke him up at 3 a.m., he told her to go away and see him at a respectable hour in the morning. Her young son was on his own a good part of the time, and some said that, teenager though he was, he was peddling drugs.

Things got worse and worse. She invited all kinds of people into her home, and sometimes there were sounds of violence. One day she came to my house and threatened to kill me or herself. I took the threat seriously and as she was then living in Sóller, I spoke to the mayor who said it was a matter for the American authorities. When I got in touch with them, I was told not to worry as they had the matter well in hand. Shortly thereafter she was ordered expelled from Spain but could not be sent out of the country till her son who was in hiding was found and reunited with her.

Vicki and her son returned to Sóller a year or so later. She was calm and apologized to me for her behaviour. She also explained that while she did not like to take medicine for her manic depression, she was now doing so. Soon, however, she began again to associate with the wrong people – at least, wrong for her – and calling attention to herself from the authorities.

She had earlier bought an old house in the center of the town but lived with little comfort as she had insufficient funds for a complete renovation. There were many complaints about her, and once again she was expelled, this time for three years.

One day I happened to read a brief article in a Spanish paper about a woman, previously a resident of Mallorca, who had been found dead in New York. Her body had been viciously bruised and slashed. I felt immediately that it was Vicki – and later her death was confirmed. The amazing fact that emerged later was that she had left her house to the town hall of Sóller. Her two sons, both now grown, contested the will but they lost the case.

A very proper English woman, Emma Bristol, widowed some years before, bought a large *finca* which she herself had difficulty in managing. Fortunately, she became attracted to a conductor on the trolley to the port and he to her. Soon they became a pair and Xim took over many of the responsibilities of the property. She spoke almost no Spanish and he, at first, no English; they communicated in French in which, like many Mallorquíns, he was fluent and she barely so. Emma took Xim to England a few times and introduced him as a "conductor," leaving her friends to draw the wrong conclusion. We all thought highly of Xim but one night he surprised me. I had been to a party in Fornalutx and walked back to Sóller with Rosa, Carla and Xim – Emma was in England. The two women dropped off at their house and Xim accompanied me to mine. Out of the blue he gently propositioned me. It had never occurred to me that he was interested, and I just as gently turned him down. After all, Emma was a friend of mine, but if she had not been .... who knows?

After some years together they decided to move to another part of the island, a decision not easy for him as it meant giving up his job and pension rights. When she bought the land and built their new house, Emma put everything into Xim's name; this eliminated a lot of the red tape that she as a foreigner would have had to cope with. In addition, he was younger than she and might very well outlive her so would have no inheritance tax to pay. It did not work out that way, however, as he developed health problems and died in his 60's. Under his will she, of course, inherited, but as they had not been married (she would have lost her British pension if they had been), the inheritance tax would have been heavy. Luckily she was able to prove that they had lived together some thirty years, so she was recognized as his common-law wife.

Emma returned to Sóller where she lived quietly with her dogs and her garden until her late 90's. She was never sick and never hospitalized except for one night. When she was 96 or 97, however, she could not manage alone and went to live in a nursing home in England. I heard that at 98 she had a "boy friend", another resident at the home, but she died shortly thereafter.

An elderly Swiss-American couple rented a house I looked after in La Huerta. They were obviously very devoted to each other. On the morning they were to leave for the United States, I received a message that one of them had died so I rushed to the house. Pierre was crying. He had awakened to find his wife lying dead next to him. Marie had died of a massive heart attack. He was much older than she and not in the best of health and certainly had thought that she would outlast him. The poor man was desolate. They had been married for many years, and as they had no children each had depended on the other. Though he was half blind, he decided to stay on with the help of a woman friend, and all of us did what we could for him. It soon became obvious, however, that he could not possibly cope on his own, and eventually he agreed to go back to the States where he had a cousin who would help him.

Pierre gave me some money to have a stone carved with the single word LOVE to be placed on his wife's grave. We corresponded for some years and he occasionally sent some funds for the upkeep of the grave. Finally his eyesight failed completely, and some time later a letter arrived advising me of his death. To the best of my knowledge, there is now no one else left here who knows who is buried under that stone though there are surely cemetery records.

Another foreign *fornaluxenc,* an Australian, was a professor of Spanish at a Canadian university. He had first come to spend holidays in the 40's or early 50's. Through the years he bought ruins until he owned five in Fornalutx, all of which he gradually rebuilt with imaginative touches that maintained the local character of construction. Eventually he sold most of them, keeping only one house and a cottage for his own and friends' use. He was a great cook and I always was pleased to have a dinner invitation, never knowing in advance whether we'd be dining on Oriental, South American or Mallorquín food.

We were all so different from each other and also different from the Mallorquíns; but as long as we behaved ourselves publicly, they accepted us and were tolerant of our foibles. It would not have been surprising if many of the local people who had passed through very hard times during and after the Civil War had been resentful of all these foreigners with what seemed to them a lot of money. What really raised hackles was the exclamation of some visitors when buying something, "Oh, how cheap!"

Unfortunately, not all the visitors did behave well. Perhaps the most embarrassing conversation I ever had took place after two men, one of them quite well known in the musical and theatrical world in London, made love one afternoon on the terrace of the house next to mine, in full view of the owners of the estate opposite, who threatened to call the *Guardia Civil*. I had arranged the let to these two men so had the unpleasant task of telling them that they might do what they wanted indoors but certainly not in view of neighbors or passersby. Our relationship after that was cold, to say the least, and I was considerably relieved when they left shortly afterwards.

But while there may have been and are differences between the local people and the foreigners, in one field, at least, they may be very similar. Politicians seem to be the same everywhere; they look for public exposure and publicity. There is a Mallorquín political figure who shall be nameless who manages to get her name and/or picture in the newspapers almost every day. Some of the mention is not favourable, but I have a feeling that that does not bother her much. She even wrote me a letter of congratulations once, presumably a form letter, when I had a bit of publicity as a blood donor.

Another successful woman politician is someone I met once or twice many years ago at a meeting of a charitable group. Since then I have come across her a couple of times and have deliberately with tongue in cheek greeted her effusively using her name, to see what her reaction would be. We have always embraced and exchanged a few words, but I am positive that she does not have any idea who I am. I have to admit that I would not do it if she were of the political party I support here.

I have always loved dogs and cats and I greet any I meet on the street. In fact, I first met Rosa because I stopped to speak to her big dog and then realized that it would be rude not to address the person. A year after I moved to Can Bessó, the American airman and his wife who lived above me were transferred to a base in Germany, and I inherited Smokey, a beautiful one-year-old blue-gray cat. She lived with me in Sóller and Fornalutx till she was eighteen, stopped eating and drinking water and began to weaken. After some days I sadly took her to the vet to end her life as I was afraid that in jumping from one roof to another she might fall and hurt herself.

My next cat, Feroz, was not really ferocious; but when I gave her as a young kitten a little food and the mother tried to take it, the baby spat at her. Neither cat was mine – the mother was fed by a couple of neighbors. One night when the kitten was a few months old, I took her into my house and let her sleep on the bed, but only for one night, I said to myself. Naturally, the next day I could not put her out, and I felt guilty when her mother came to look for her. Feroz lived with me until she was nineteen, but then her mind seemed to go, and one night she went out and never returned. I missed her enormously as she had been a great comfort to me during a low period in my life. I decided no more cats.

A month later, however, in 1999, I saw an advertisement offering a four-year-old affectionate Siamese who needed a good home. I called immediately. End result: The next day I brought Whiskey home. He was upset and nervous and scratched me badly that night. "All right," I said, "I am not having a vicious animal. Back you go tomorrow," and went to bed. An hour later, I relented and went downstairs to see him. He came toward me and licked my hand. That did it. He won – well, we both did as he has been with me ever since. P.S. After a year or so I decided that the name Whiskey did not do him justice; and as I wanted to change it to something that he would still recognize, it seemed obvious to make it Whiskers. But perhaps this name came to the fore from my subconscious as later I remembered the toy fox terrier I had been given when I was eleven or twelve, whose name was Whiskers also.

Whiskers has been joined by a female Siamese named Chatka. They do not care much for each other but do not quarrel. Except in hot weather, they both sleep with me, one on each side.

While I am a cat lover, however, I do not believe that I would have arrived from New York with nine cats, two of them crippled, as an American woman did in 1961. She planned to stay for six months and could not leave any of them behind. Her funds were limited so she was not too pleased when on arrival in Spain she had to pay import duty of thirty-five per cent on the value of her pets that she had arbitrarily declared on leaving. It was probably just as well that she did not stay longer as she was indiscreet about her affair with the local carpenter, a married man with a young child, as a result of which her Mallorquín neighbors turned against her. She duly left taking her nine cats with her.

Having worked for the polio foundation for many years in New York, I found it natural to devote time to one or two non-profit organizations in Spain, so when the officers of the English Speaking Residents Association (ESRA), which was formed in Mallorca in 1980 or so, came out to Sóller to organize a local area group, I became a member of the Board and in charge of social services. The whole idea of private charitable organizations was almost unknown in Spain at that time. There was Caritas of the Church, the Red Cross, Cancer and a few others, but most Spaniards knew nothing of the numerous non-profit groups that operate in Great Britain and the United States, and acting as a volunteer to help was not widespread here. Until fairly recently families had been large, and there was always an aunt or single daughter to help out at home. The tax authorities did not even recognize the non-profit-making aspect of such groups.

In 1988 the president of ESRA, Jim Arnold-Boakes, and his wife Judy, who was a very active Board member, left the organization to establish Overseas Association: Social and Information Services (O.A.S.I.S.). I became very involved in their work; and when I was elected president, I resigned from ESRA Later on O.A.S.I.S., under the presidency of Judy, became Age Concern Spain, then the federation Age Concern España with organisations on the three principal Balearic Islands and on the mainland. As financial controller, I worked closely with Judy and Jim, and my activities became more and more time-consuming. Occasionally I visited one of our associations on the other islands or on the mainland. By this time, of course, I was officially retired as I could not have devoted so many hours a week to AC if I had still been actively earning a living.

Finally in 2003 I decided that it was time to devote myself to a project I had had in mind for years because I knew that if I did not get to it soon, it would be too late, the project being this book. I rather sadly turned in my resignation from the Board of Age Concern though I still do a bit of writing for the quarterly magazine..

TRAVELING

One of the reasons I had decided when I first came here to learn Castilian and not Mallorquín (Catalan) –- I could not do both at the same time -- was that I hoped one day to travel around the mainland and wanted to be fluent in a language known to all Spaniards. Although I had been off the island a few times during the 60's to see my family in the United States and other times to visit Paris and Barcelona, it was not until 1969 that I began my exploration of the peninsula. My good friend Boris and I took our motorbikes on the ferry to Valencia, known as the City of Towers, where it was pouring on our arrival, so we headed for the canteen at the dock, indulging in *conacs* and snacks for the next few hours.

The rain did not stop so we finally made a dash for the city center and, drenched as we were, agreed on the first accommodation we could find in a modest hotel where the rooms though sparsely furnished were comfortable enough except that the toilets were outside on little balconies. One night it rained heavily and water cascaded down the stairways from the roof. Surprisingly enough, in the mornings we saw well-dressed young men with briefcases leaving the hotel on the way to their offices. Their appearance gave the impression that they could have afforded a better place to live.

186

We toured the eastern provinces, one time putting our motorbikes on a train (we had to drain every drop of fuel from the vehicles before they were allowed on) from one city to another. As our funds were limited, we slept in simple hotels or inns and ate modestly; I had my first taste of garlic soup one evening and that was enough. I think garlic in moderation is a great addition to many dishes, but a whole plateful of it is not my idea of a good way to start a dinner. Obviously Spaniards and others disagree with me.

Boris was a great traveling companion and never complained about anything. We saw the famous Hanging Houses of Terruel and many other picturesque and historic sites. On our return to Valencia, we were forced to return to our first hotel, no other rooms being available as an international congress was taking place in the city.

Over the years I have gone around the mainland by car a number of times, visiting a good part of Spain and Portugal. While I did a lot of traveling alone in Europe – my Mallorquín friends and neighbors seemed amazed that I would make such trips unaccompanied – I sometimes went with a friend. In the early 1990's I met Micky and we went together to Peru, India, Indonesia and Thailand and twice to Sri Lanka, where we experienced the tsunami on December 26, 2004, from which we were exceedingly lucky to escape unscathed. But I should not like to live through a repetition of the event.

The following year we visited Thailand (my second time there) and Indonesia, spending quite some weeks on Bali.. For me the most striking moment was when I faced three komodo dragons in the wild on the island of that name – and they really are three meters long and flesh-eaters.

My last visit to the United States, my ninth, took place in 1992, and I do not expect to go back again. Altogether since 1959 I have left Mallorca eighty times, not including brief visits to other parts of the country on behalf of the charitable groups with which I was working.

While I shall not include details of my various holidays and trips away, two experiences make interesting reading. On a tour of Europe in 1973 with a group of Spaniards, we spent a few days in Budapest. Our guide told us that there was nothing of interest to buy so there was not much point in exchanging a lot of money for Hungarian *forints*. As I do not like to be herded around with a group, I wandered through the city alone as I did wherever we went. I was fortunate, though, to have an introduction to someone who took me to the ballet one night.

On my way back to the hotel on our final day I spotted a newsstand and made a beeline for it because my sister-in-law, a professor of education, who had a fine collection of international children's books, had asked me to look for some while I was there as her library lacked any in Hungarian. I eagerly selected three or four and held out the few remaining coins I had to the smiling woman – unfortunately the only words I knew in Hungarian were "please" and "thank you." Alas, even the cheapest book cost sixteen *forints* and I had only fourteen, so I reluctantly put them all down. She, however, in dumb show indicated that I could have the one for that amount. I took it but rushed to the hotel and changed another couple of dollars, then back to the now closed newsstand just in time to catch the owner before she left. We were both delighted when I bought three more books and paid her in full.

On that same tour we unexpectedly stopped at the Nazi death camp Mauthausen. We were taken through and shown horrifying pictures and instruments of torture, accompanied by a verbal description of what had taken place. My Spanish companions were completely silent until suddenly as we left, a woman burst out, "What beasts!"

Others chimed in and one or two of my companions began to cry. These people, still living under Franco, had literally never heard about the extermination camps. Censorship had seen to that.

LOOKING BACK

It may be hard for those who have not during these past fifty years experienced the changes in the quality of life, the enormous amount of construction and rise in the cost of living in Mallorca to comprehend just how overwhelming they were. Inflation has run rampant just as in many other holiday destinations. The introduction of the euro in January, 2002, caused an almost immediate increase in prices. Previously the government had assured the public that prices would not rise, but they did. For example, many an item that had cost one hundred pesetas was now priced at one euro, or a little more than one hundred and sixty-six pesetas. Tourists and residents alike have complained. And this year a good part of the excellent orange crop of Fornalutx was not picked as market prices were not high enough to cover the cost of labor.

Changes have obviously taken place everywhere but far more gradually than here where tourism has had such a tremendous effect. My little village of some seven hundred inhabitants (there were fewer than six hundred when I moved here in 1971) now has an apartment-hotel, for which fruit trees had to be uprooted, as well as three or four other small hotels, none of which is cheap. Young people cannot afford to buy

190

and/or build housing, so many continue to live in their parents' homes. (There is some reasonable government housing but it is not sufficient.) And the owls and nightingales which I used to hear have disappeared as more houses were built on the hillside. The road between Sóller and its port was lined with beautiful leafy plane trees, so that even in summer the walk to the port was pleasant. But as the number of cars in the valley increased and more tourist buses came out from the Palma airport, the authorities decided to widen the road – and to do so the trees had to be cut down. Very sad for the residents whose protests were not heard.

A regular contributor to the Majorca Daily Bulletin, Luis Ripoll, wrote in April, 1964, that, "At the end of Calle 31 Diciembre you are already in the countryside," (this is now in the center of Palma) and "Palma fortunately does not have those ugly suburbs that disfigure so many European cities." Were he to see Palma today he would probably have a heart attack.

In 1974 a Professor Guillermo Miralles, newly returned after ten years' absence, stated that in two decades, Mallorca had jumped from "almost medieval times" to a modern world tourist resort. Needless to say, many people here resented being told that twenty years before they had been living under medieval conditions even though it was true that there had been enormous lacks.

The twentieth century saw enormous growth in the populations of Palma, Mallorca and the Balearic Islands. For example, at the end of 1900 there were 311,650 inhabitants on the islands, which rose by the last day of 1950 to 441,730. Since then the population has increased in leaps and bounds, and on December 31, 2003, it was 947,361, of which 126,505 were foreigners. By now it has surely passed the one million mark, and the national population exceeds forty-three million.

Sóller and Fornalutx have also shown increases. While the latter is forty-ninth out of fifty-three Mallorquín municipalities in number of inhabitants, it with three others has the highest percentage of foreigners. Incidentally, the Catholic Monarchs Isabel and Fernando ordered what was probably the first count in Spain of households in 1492 in the provinces of Castille.

Another figure which shows how far Mallorca has come up in the world in recent years is Palma's Son San Joan airport's twelfth position among the busiest airports in Europe with regard to passengers; there were 19,000,000 in 2003. Compare that figure with the 40,000 people who visited Mallorca in 1935 and the 677,000 in 1963.

In addition, eight hundred and ninety-six obsolete hotels were closed during 1990 to 2005, chiefly one- and two-star establishments, to be replaced by six hundred and ninety three-, four- and five-star hotels. More than a third of the homes in the Balearics are now on the Internet, and almost a half have a computer. Our newspapers and authorities boast of the many wealthy and prominent foreign pop stars, businessmen and others who have bought properties in recent years, such as, Claudia Schiffer, Boris Becker and Michael Douglas.

Of course, with economic growth has come the spread of supermarkets and shopping centers, which has led to the disappearance of a great many small family-run local shops which could not compete. I read recently that the oldest shop in Palma, which had been in existence for almost five hundred years, was on the point of closing; but this was due to the

192

fact that all of the owner brothers and sisters are in the 70's and have no descendants. No one wants to take on such a business – a shame as I used to go there occasionally to buy rope and all kinds of basketware and woven goods.

During Franco's era his name and/or photo appeared on the first or second page of Spanish newspapers almost every day. Within thirty days of his death there was little mention of him; two months later he had more or less disappeared from the daily press. After democracy began to take hold, most of the local town halls renamed all the streets and avenues with Francoist names; but it was not until a Socialist government was elected in conservative Fornalutx that Calle Franco became Carrer de sa Plaça.

The political and civil rights picture is completely different from what it was during Franco's regime when there were no elections, i.e., from 1936 onwards. He died in November, 1975 after which conditions began to change. There had been one referendum in that long period and voting was compulsory. Voters' names were checked off lists, and those who did not have a valid excuse for not voting, such as illness, lost some of their social security benefits. Ballots were not confidential and the only way to avoid voting for the Caudillo, which few people dared to take, was to spoil the ballot in some way.

The first free elections in forty-one years took place on the fifteenth of June, 1977, the winners being the Democratic Center party; and no one under the age of sixty-two had ever voted freely before. Some of the new candidates for office in the Balearics and on the mainland had been imprisoned under

Franco. But not everyone was happy at political developments, at least in my village. When I said to a young woman before this first election that surely everyone must be delighted to be able to vote for the candidate of her choice, she said, "Ah, *señora*, under Franco we had peace for forty years." True enough, but at what cost?

One morning toward the end of February, 1981, I received a call from a friend in Germany who asked me about the rightwing coup taking place in Spain. I was flabbergasted as I knew nothing about it, not having listened to or seen any news that morning or the evening before. For some hours while the conspirators held the Parliament, the situation was very tricky and it appeared that the five-year-old democracy was in serious trouble; but the King acted very decisively and bravely, order was soon restored and the crisis terminated.

In May of that year in Barcelona two hundred hostages were taken in a bank by twenty armed men who threatened that all of the two hundred would be killed if Colonel Tejero, who had led the coup in February, and his associates were not released from prison. Fortunately the group was arrested before it could carry out its threats.

Amnesty International reported recently that approximately thirty thusand people disappeared after being arrested during the Civil War and Franco's almost forty years of rule. It must be remembered also that both sides in the war, the legally elected Republicans and the Francoist Nationalist rebels, perpetrated atrocities. In spite of all the improvements in freedom of movement and civil rights, as late as July, 2005, many political victims of Franco's regime and/or their families had not received recompense.

At my age I would find it extremely difficult, if not impossible, to live as we did in the 50's and 60's. And remember, most of us at that time had come from surroundings where we enjoyed all sorts of physical comforts that were lacking here, all of which we had willingly foregone in exchange for the advantages Mallorca gave us. For me, the minuses included the fact that to earn a living meant very long hours six or seven days a week during many years. But in the United States, too, I had been a workaholic, so being healthy and young enough, I could cope with my hard schedule. The plus side included fresh air and a good diet, many strong friendships with people of varied backgrounds and interests, magnificent surroundings and a loosening of the emotional rigidity which had governed my previous life. I am today a far different person from the one who first set eyes on Mallorca in 1955, and I consider that I am among the fortunate of this world.

Not only have I never regretted my decision to come to live and to remain on this beautiful island, but looking back over ninety-one years I can reiterate that that decision was the best one I have made during my lifetime.